A SAD STORY MADE HIM RICH

Leonard Mukuka (also known as) Leon Khurks

If you purchase this book without a cover, or purchase PDF, JPG or Tiff copy of this book, it is likely a stolen property. With that said, neither of the Authors, publishers or employees have received any payments for the type of copy you received in that format.

We urge you to please not purchase any kind of such copy And to instantly report anyone selling that kind of copy to www.winwithleon.com directly to Leon's support by contacting the support through the provided way or either via his Social Media support team.

Facebook
@Leonard Mukuka

"A Sad Story Made Him Rich is a starting point for everyone who wants to escape poverty and become Financially Free."

A SAD STORY MADE HIM RICH

Contents

CHAPTERS

1. BORN IN THE VILLAGE
2. GOING TO THE CITY
3. LIVING IN POVERTY
4. ESCAPING POVERTY

5. JOURNEY TO FINANCIAL FREEDOM

6. MAKING MONEY WORK FOR YOU

7. A JOB CAN'T GIVE FINANCIAL FREEDOM

8. BUILDING A BUSINESS

9. IMPORTANCE OF ENTREPRENEURSHIP

10. STAYING RICH FOREVER

INTRODUCTION

A Sad Story Made Him Rich is Leon's story of growing up poor and living in poverty — his real life from the village and how he struggled throughout his earliest stage of life from childhood to where he Learned Lessons of life. It has talked about how he lived in poverty— and the ways in which his life of living poor shaped his thoughts about Education, money, time investment, money investing and Managing Money to become Financially Free and Stable. It also talks about how he Escaped poverty and live a meaningful life, Turning poverty into success. The book explodes the myth that you need to earn a high income to be rich and explains the difference between working for money and having to manage your money so that you make it work for you.

When you start managing your finances, you'll have a better perspective of where and how you're spending your money. This can help you keep within your budget, and even increase your savings. With good personal finance management, you'll also learn to control your money so you can achieve your financial goals.

It's important to learn the ins and outs of money management from a young age. Teaching Yourself about finance and money management will help You to save and spend sensibly in later life.

Whether or not you have a financial background, you will need some sort of money management skills in your daily life. Learning finance at the university does not guarantee you to be good at money management. Many people are struggling everyday or during some period of time with managing their money,

Understanding a full picture of your finances will help you have a better plan for your future and ensure your life is secured financially.

Throughout the story and courses of this Book, you're going to learn how to turn poverty into success, how to manage your Money, how to make money work for you and the Importance of Entrepreneurship, Take your time to Read and Explore Financial Freedom.

CHAPTER 1

BORN IN THE VILLAGE

Once upon a time, a child was born in a dark place, with no electricity light, but only candle light. His parents lived in a village at a farm which was very far from other village places.

To estimate, if you want to find the next farm you have to move about 20 kilometers from their farm to find the next. Nevertheless they loved their home still.

However, the new born baby was a very handsome and healthy bouncing baby boy. His mother was very happy to receive him, so did his father too.

Telling other people and other family members about the new born baby was not easy due to the above reasons as they lived in far places.

At that time, no one at home had a phone not even the father, "No" vehicle only one old bicycle. The family was struggling financially, but still they lived very happy.

A week later.

The child was Growing and everyone continued to speak of his arrival to the world called earth. The day came when they asked his father to give him a name.

"We will call him Friday." His father said with a smile.

"No that's a weird name." His mother replied.

They struggled to find a best name so they chose to go think about it. On the next day, his father came back from a Vegetable Garden he cultivated. With a Smiling face he said:

"Honey! I have found a perfect and suitable name for our son." Telling his wife.

"Ooh, tell me about it." His wife replied.

"His Name is: **Leonard.** How is that Honey?"

"Wow so brilliant it suits him and sounds great. And For me I will call him **Leon.**" Wife says.

Mukuka was the son's Surname. A lot of people heard the news about the baby's new Name and began to use it. Some called him **Leonard** and others called him **Leon.**

This is how my life began. I was born on February 23/1998. My life didn't begin in a Rich family that had everything they needed but they did the best of all I can appreciate to provide me with all I needed. Am so Thankful to my Mom and Dad, *Rachel* & *Alfred* for doing all the best they did.

I continued to live in the same place without Electricity only using fire when we need light at night. I never knew how Electricity looked like, never tested porridge for babies as my mother used other village methods to provide my food when she stopped breastfeeding me.

Years Later

I was growing up and learning things, my brain was capturing every bit of information and storing it deep within.

I was 6 Years this time and I still had never seen Electricity, Cars, phone as well as a TV. We still lived in the same village where even a vehicle can't pass. There were no big Roads, many people and school Nearby.

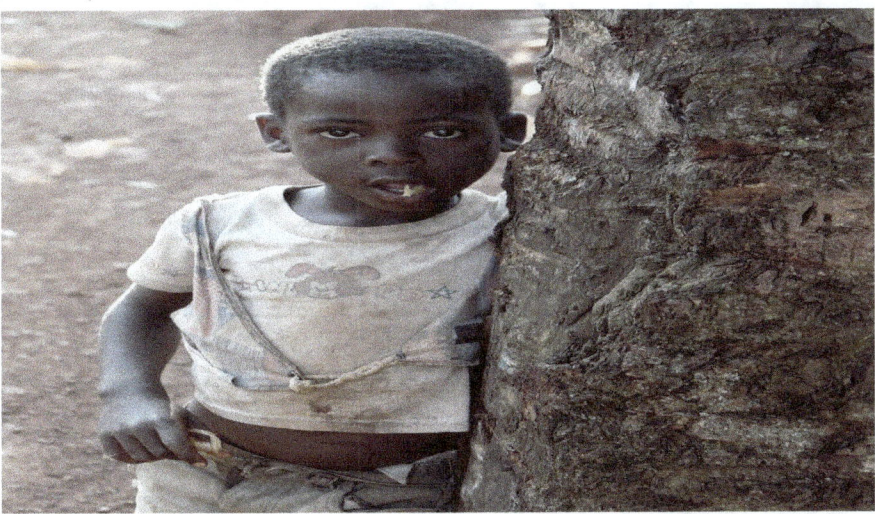

However, my parents thought I needed to go to school, so they sent me to go and live with my Grandparents who lived a bit nearby to the location of the School.

I went to my grandpa's house and it was cool, "Yes it was", Because I thought I'll be able to see a car, TV or Electricity. Guess what; what I thought never happened. Still I never got a chance to see all those because my grandparents were also in the village. Only that they lived near to the school.

Every evening, I used to sit alone looking at the beautiful stars in the sky. I used to imagine the Stars and Moon as Electricity light, never knew how all these things looked like.

In the afternoon I could Go to my Grandpa's fishponds to watch the fish, and Looking at the waters. Seeing myself in the water, Made me feel like am watching the TV. I could sit there for a long period of time talking to myself and imagining things.

When children learn new skills, they also build independence, confidence and self-esteem. So helping children learn new skills can be an important part of supporting overall development too.

My Grandfather had seen an airplane before, he used to tell me about it and how beautiful it looks. "You should focus on school my Grandson, so that you become a pilot and fly a plane." Grandpa says

Starting school

They Enrolled me as a grade one (1) pupil at Chilekwa Mwanba Basic School based in Zambia, Kasama. I was very happy because at this point, I was fully convinced that I'll now start learning how to become a pilot, as my vision was to fly a plane just like my Grandfather told me.

I already knew how to Read, Write as well as Counting before I even went to school. My parents had already taught me how to read.

I was so focused on school and I was waiting for the day my teacher could teach me how to fly a plane, but still we had not reached that subject yet.

I didn't have a bag, so I used to carry books in a plastic bag, I could remember the time I used to go to school with no shoes. My school was very far from where I lived, but I was still managing because I really want to succeed on my goal of becoming a pilot.

Nevertheless, every time I come back from school, I watched Birds flying in the sky, from one tree to another, I could vision myself flying on a plane each time I see a Bird flying. I never saw an airplane even this time, my Grandpa only told me about it.

The Next day at school I asked my teacher the day we will start learning about airplanes and how to fly them. He looked at me and said:

""Son. why do you need to learn that at your Age?

"Because I want to be a pilot and make my Grandfather proud." I said.

"This is not the time to learn that Son. Grow up, continue learning the syllabus course's, If you continue and stay focused, you'll make it happen and your Grandfather will be proud of you Son." My teacher said.

That day I came back home with big smiles in my face, I told my grandpa about it and he was happy too.

I could read books, answer my homework's and Getting everything Good. My parents where proud of my work at school and my good understandings. I never wanted to fail, because if I fail school, I'll never be a pilot and I'll never be successful. So all the time, I had was spent little grade one (1) books, stories and many funny stuffs.

I still used to be alone and look at the stars because I really wanted to see electricity as I was reading and answering my home work using candle light at night.

We struggled Financially, so my parents thought they should change a living by shifting from the village to town. When I heard the news I was so excited, because I knew I'll see everything I wanted to see if this happens.

Plans were working and moving very smooth, so my family had to shift from their farm. They came to live in my grandfathers compound to prepare themselves for a new living.

I was very happy, I left grandpa's house and started living with my parents again. I continued to go to school and everyone was supporting me. Though I never had a bag, they made sure my plastic bag and books are intact before I leave.

At this point I never had shoes. I was going to school still, because my mother told me she'll get me a shoe as soon as they get the money.

I was focused I never wanted to stop going to school, because I new school is everything I needed to become successful. My teacher was so good and Kind to me, he made sure I learn everything, so I was among the best pupils in Class all because of my vision and Goal of being a pilot. If not because of that; I don't know if I would have focused.

My father was working hard preparing for everything we needed so that we can go to another city.

We were happy, I couldn't wait to go. I really wanted to see a car and watch TV. I had never been to town before, so I didn't even know how it looked like. We lived in a very small grass Thatched house, so it wasn't easy for me to guess the kind of houses that are found in town.

Plans Of Going To Town

My father cultivated a very big garden of onions, cabbages and many vegetables to prepare the money that was needed for moving to another city.

While all those were growing, he started a business dealing with fish. He used to move a distance to go and get dry fish and put it in the market for selling.

However, he had no vehicle so he used his bicycle to get everything done. When coming back he could walk the all day sometimes two days to just get home.

He never had a phone so my mother couldn't communicate with him, not even the family could. We were just waiting and never knowing when he will come back.

This was so scaring because we wouldn't know if he Was attacked or rather killed. But God was protecting him and we could see him come back home with more fish than we ever expected.

He worked so hard. Even my mother was so hard working that we were not Lacking anything. When I see all these, I was asking myself Why a man and woman that never finished school managed to be happy and do business that gave them what they needed. They did everything under their terms and conditions.

I had many questions that I needed to be answered, so next day at school, I asked my teacher a question.

"Sir. Can one be happy and successful without school?" I asked.

"No. For Education is the key to Success.! Continue working hard and learning son, this is the way to achieve everything you need." He said.

Honestly, I was totally confused at this point. I was trying to connect what he told me, with the life my parents had lived and I concluded and believed to say, Education is the key. "Yes it is, but in this book we will see the type of education." I continued and was so focused at this time.

My father was focused, he did everything possible and at this moment he managed to have some money saved to start a new life.

My mother's sister was Married to a very handsome Man **Nick,** who lived in a different city of "Ndola" based in Copperbelt Zambia.

He came to the village to pick up his wife and take her to his city. When he came, he asked my father if he would like to go start a new life also in his city Ndola.

This is what me, my father and the all family wanted. He was excited to receive the offer and he couldn't hesitate to take it.

"YES. And for the past few months my family and I have been thinking about this." My father said.

"Okay prepare everything needed and talk to your family about it. Nick said.

He was a man of few words and looked very intelligent.

My father came home smiling and told us about the day he had with **Nick.** I was very excited, my mother was happy too.

There were Nine (9) of us in the family. The next day after school, my parents told me they wanted to speak to me. I was scared, "Yes I was," because I thought I had done something wrong. Guess what.!

"We thought about it, me and your mother and came to the conclusion that I should go with you to town, everyone will remain here in the village and we will come pick them when we establish a living in town." My father said.

I was so excited, Never said a word, I just dissolved in tears. I was so happy inside but it could not be expressed. I was worried about my mother and other siblings, but not too much, because at this point. I was fully convinced I will see everything I had dreamed of Seeing.

Importance of Learning new things as a kid that I discovered.

Children's can build great knowledge from a young age with a window of opportunity to develop into anything they love. During these early years, children are naturally intrigued as they experience everything for the first time; they are constantly absorbing new information and quickly able to learn by example.

Being able to develop your child's ability through engaging them with learning when they are young and curious sets great foundations for their future.

Learning Can Boost self-confidence.

Quicker speed when tackling questions.

Ability to think differently by looking at the bigger picture.

Ability to solve problems in day to day life.

Considering this, I found something that helped me grow in my early childhood which can also help you, or your children's. And that is:

Drawing and painting pictures – can inspire creativity and greater expression of feelings.

Building blocks of different shapes and sizes – can help with recognizing different patterns, putting things in order and developing a sense of judgement.

Number, word, and picture cards – can help them familiarize with an object but also become a visual learner. A good memory will certainly help them throughout later exams.

Reading to, or with, your child – widens their vocabulary by introducing them to new words. Before you know it, they could be picking out their favorite book to read to you.

Though I never had all of those, during my research I found that it works so well and it helps a child grow their brain.

By exploring different activities and ways of learning with your child you can see which learning methods suit them best, as well as where their passion lies. You should try to make their learning exciting and interactive, not only to keep them engaged and have the greatest impact, but additionally to further develop your shared bond.

Starting primary school is a big transition for young children, however, by introducing learning into their daily routine in advance, you can give them a head start, meaning they'll likely adjust quickly and get their academic experience off to a flying start. Together your efforts will help ensure they begin school with boosted confidence in their skills and ability and aren't afraid to tackle harder work. This confidence and positive, can-do attitude will then carry into their daily life with whatever challenges they may face. The earlier they learn, the better.

Across the world, thousands of young learners are currently thriving on math's and English programmes. It is very easy now days to find better learning than it was in my days of childhood.

Watching your child flourish from an infant to an adult is certainly a great privilege and what is instilled in them at an early age will be of great value to their future.

Sadly I Was rolled out of school because I had to move in with my Father to another city. We didn't get a transfer, but my parents told my teacher and headmaster that I will stop going to school because I will be leaving the village soon.

My teacher was very sad, Nevertheless he encouraged me to continue on my journey of Learning so that I become a pilot.

"The Only way you'll be successful, is through school. Never stop focusing Kid." He concluded and we shake hands.

CHAPTER 2

GOING TO THE CITY

It is a Beautiful evening, I am so happy and prepared to go. Our bags are packed only waiting to leave tomorrow morning. I couldn't wait to see a car tomorrow that will take us to town.

After having a dream of a very big car chasing me, I woke up and I was scared, I didn't sleep, but still I couldn't wait to Go.

The next nice morning, Nick and his wife are prepared, my uncle comes with his bicycle to Carry our luggage. Dad Hug my mother for a Goodbye, I do the same and everyone is sad but happy that we're going to start a new life.

On the 1 November 2009 the journey began. We started coming to town and after walking for 4 hours, I just heard a sound, I was asking my father what that was but he told me to wait and see for myself.

I just saw a very big road, and after a minute, Wow I saw a car for the first time, it wasn't so big because it was a old car.

When we moved towards the vehicle I was scared of entering inside because I've never been on a car before.

For the first time, I was on the car and we started to move. After moving a distance, I saw some cables and poles. I never wanted to ask, I never knew what they were.

"Do you know what this is?" My father asked.

"No!" what are these?

At this time my father explained Electricity to me and as we moved along the way to town, I could see electricity in houses.

But this moment we were still in a village town, and not Ndola where Nick lived.

We Arrived in town and I can see cars, Electricity and a lot of houses near to one another, different from where I lived.

We slept in this town waiting for a bus which was coming the next day, that was supposed to take us to the city.

The next morning at 06:30am I saw a very big bus, I looked very small, my Father had to lift me to get me inside, as I was still a kid by then.

When I entered the bus, I saw two small Glasses, guess what it was. It was TV screen, I never knew how it looked like. As the bus started to move, they turned on the TV and I was so happy seeing a TV on a bus for the first time.

I grew up so poor and with a poor mindset as I never saw those advanced technologies and things.

Growing up poor can influence people's sense of control and in turn may lead them to more impulsive decision-making and quickly giving up on challenging tasks in uncertain situations.

Two people with different childhood backgrounds are likely to respond to uncertainty in different ways, even if as adults they have a similar socioeconomic status. I discovered that adults who grew up poor were more inclined to consider difficult and uncertain living conditions as beyond their control, while those from affluent backgrounds found them to be within their control. This leads to different reactions to the same situation.

Differing perceptions of control affected whether people were able to postpone a reward, with people from poorer backgrounds behaving more impulsively in uncertain situations than those from wealthy families. In addition, after recalling personal financial hardship and then being asked to solve a difficult puzzle, those who grew up poor can give up much sooner than those who grew up wealthy, even if they had similar incomes as adults.

Persistence is directly tied to myriad important outcomes, including self-control, academic achievement, substance abuse, criminal behavior, healthy eating and overspending.

Growing up poor can teach you valuable lessons that will help you become better at making, spending, and saving money as you get older. You might not realize or appreciate these lessons at the time, and you could think that poverty is the worst thing to ever happen to you. But looking back now, I've realized that growing up poor was probably a good thing.

If you come from a poor background, the numerous success stories of people who managed to escape poverty and become who they are now should motivate you to view your situation; not as an obstacle but as an opportunity to learn and succeed. You only need to have the right mindset and be willing to learn and put in the effort to escape poverty.

We took the all day long just going to the city. I was very happy and excited to be on the bus but Still I was tired because it moved the all day long.

We reached to the city and guess what, it was very beautiful than I ever imagined. We reached at night. I could not see stars when I looked up to the sky. I was only seeing Bulbs of Electricity on buildings. This was the happiest moment of my life.

Nick took us to his brothers house to spend a night there before we could go to his house as it was far and it was already late.

The next morning I went outside to see the view of the town houses, but I got confused. I got confused, because well you know the Sun seemed to be coming from an apposite direction. I saw things opposite so I thought like am going crazy. I can remember running back inside the house and everyone is asking me.

" What's Wrong Kid!" Nick's brother asked.

" Well, am scared, Why is the Sun coming from this direction?" I said.

"Ooooh. Don't be scared it's just that you've moved a far distance and you're tired. Brush your teeth and get some rest.

I went on and I did what he said. I was still puzzled, I never understood anything.

Around 2pm we were prepared to Go to Nick's house. So we said Goodbyes to his brothers family. We took a Taxi and got on the way.

We started leaving town and went to a far compound that looked a bit like my village. I was surprised to see this because I thought we've already Reached home but we exceeded town and went to village.

The house didn't have Electricity and there was no TV. The all compound didn't have Electricity and they were using fire as well as Candle light just like in the village I lived.

This was very puzzling to me. I was confused and couldn't understand what is happening. My hopes and my faith of building a good life had to shutdown right there and then.

I didn't expect that we will be able to make it even at this time. My father was also confused.

Lessons Learned from Growing Up Poor

- **To practice gratitude**

When you have too much of something, it is not unusual for you not to think much of it and take what you have for granted. On the other hand, if you don't have a lot, you learn to value and appreciate every little thing you have because you know what it is like not to have it.

The importance of having an attitude of gratitude is one of the best lessons you could learn from growing up poor. When you become rich and successful, you will likely maintain this positive attitude and never take what you have for granted.

- **How to live frugally**

One of the incredible lessons learned from growing up poor is the art of frugal living. You learn how to do without things, spend money intentionally, and save a percentage of your income for a rainy day because you know that day will surely come if you are poor. You learn to differentiate between needs and wants, thus, opt to spend on things that add the most value to your life and forgo those that don't matter as much.

After growing up poor, you know how to get the best prices and alternatives to the items you wish to buy. You also prioritize quality over quantity because you know how much more expensive low-quality items end up being due to unsatisfactory performance, repairs, and replacements.

Learning how to live frugally is one of the best things growing up poor can teach you. You could become the best at managing your money.

- **The importance of a budget**

If you grew up in a poor family, the importance of budgeting and spending your money wisely is another incredible lesson you must have learned. You likely observed how your parents or guardians had to be careful with spending to avoid running out of money before their next incoming payment.

Since they didn't have much, they had to create a spending plan each month to ensure that all your basic needs were met. When they failed to make a budget or when they didn't have enough, they probably had to get loans, which would make your situation worse due to all the debts that needed to be repaid.

Now that you are older, you know the importance of creating a budget and sticking to it because you are aware of the consequences of running out of money before the end of the month. You also want to spend wisely in order to achieve financial freedom.

- ## To thirst for more

If you're given the chance to choose the kind of living conditions you want to grow up in, you most likely wouldn't choose poverty. After all, who would want a life where they are always lacking? Thus, one of the lessons learned from growing up poor is that it motivates you and makes you thirst for more.

You know that to escape poverty, you will need to get out of your comfort zone and put in the work required to change your situation and get the things you want. You therefore, become ambitious and goal-oriented, determined to get out of poverty and working hard to avoid ever being poor again.

- ## How to use your imagination

One of the best lessons you learn from growing up poor is how to use your imagination and think outside the box instead of wallowing in self-pity. So, you don't have money; what can you do to make some? Can you make what you want instead of buying it?

For example, when you were younger, you probably had to tap into your creative side and make your own toys or costumes because your parents couldn't afford them.

When you grow up, you will have the ability to use your imagination and come up with creative solutions whenever you have financial problems as well. When you look for them, there are always alternatives and opportunities to make some extra money. That is why you often hear people say that being poor is a choice.

- ## Resilience

Growing up poor is a tough experience. You may go days without food, live in places that no human should be living in, feel embarrassed and get bullied for going to school in torn clothes, and many more circumstances that make you doubt whether you will survive and get to adulthood. But here you are now. You somehow survived. Thus, one of the best lessons learned from growing up poor is how to build resilience.

If you ever go through a difficult time because of finances in the future, you know that you will find ways to survive because you have already experienced the worst in your earlier years. You will not give up even when life gives you lemons because you have the necessary survival skills.

- ### How to make the most of the few available resources

Since you will not be taking things for granted, other incredible lessons learned from growing up poor are how to make do with what you have, how to take care of things that are valuable to you, and how to make the most of the available resources.

For example, you could cut your expenses by reusing, reducing, repurposing, and recycling things instead of throwing them away. You could also resell items you rarely use to earn some extra cash when you are struggling financially.

You can do a lot with the little you have. Growing up poor can help you learn how to make lemonade from lemons.

- ### The importance of a support system

Another great lesson learned from growing up poor is the benefits of building a strong support system that can help you when things get bad. If you are poor with no friends or close family members, you can feel alone in the world because there is no one to help you. However, if you have family and some close friends who can help you when you are struggling financially, the experience may not be as bad.

It is true that many people will usually desert you if you are poor because they assume you only want their money. Those that remain by your side through all this are your true friends. When you grow up poor, you learn to value such people and do everything you can to keep them in your life by staying in touch and supporting them whenever they need you as well.

Additionally, growing up in a low-income household with only your siblings and parents to count on makes you learn teamwork and how to share what you have. It helps in strengthening your bonds with each other.

- ## Comparison is harmful to you

When you don't have much, it is natural to feel envious if you compare your situation with others who have more. However, this social comparison can harm you as it could make you feel unhappy and dissatisfied with your life and may even lead to mental health issues such as depression. It could also result in you engaging in criminal activities while looking for a shortcut to get the riches and lifestyle you covet.

Almost everyone will seem to be in a better situation than you when you are poor. To survive, you must learn how dangerous comparison can be and focus on looking for legal ways to escape poverty instead.

If you want to be happy and satisfied with your life, stop comparing yourself with other people. Accept that there will always be someone who is doing better than you. Even when you become rich.

- ## It is okay to seek and accept help

Being poor and having to ask for or accept help from charities and other people can feel horrible. But what other choice do you have? Die from starvation? Sleep in the cold? Growing up poor teaches you to be humble and seek or accept help if you want to survive. Knowing when to admit you need help is a valuable lesson you can use even when older whenever you are struggling financially or mentally.

Growing up poor doesn't have to be the worst experience of your life. If you are willing to, you can learn many lessons from growing up poor which you can use to improve your current life and feel more fulfilled. If you are currently in poverty, don't lose hope. Stay strong and keep working hard to change your situation. The above lessons I learned from growing up poor can help you change your mindset about poverty and motivate or inspire you.

Three weeks in town

We were living just okay and with no stress. Though we never had Good food, we were not stressing to live with Nick. Nick's house was built in the same plot with his mother. So we lived with her too and I called her my Grandmother.

But things began to change everyday, and after a month, we started struggling to find food. Life became worse, my Father's money was finished trying to take care of me and himself.

We didn't start a new living and yet we continued living with Nick and his family. I felt crazy this time, Because my dream of being a pilot was already shutting down due to my father not having money for taking me back to school.

I felt really Bad at this moment and I never knew what was going to happen next. We continued suffering just like it was in the village, and it was more good in the village Because my father can start doing Gardening and make some money. But in this compound, there were no means of doing all this.

I could remember seeing my father stressed and depressed. It was bad, because we'll you know, I was still a kid and couldn't do anything to help him. To my side I was also thinking so much, and with the issue of not going to school, I was over stressed.

I could see kids of my age going to school when am just in the village, and to myself, this made me feel like it's the end of my world. I couldn't picture myself on a plane no more.

I was asking myself what my Grandpa would say if he found out. I was sad that I could sit alone the all day as I never had friends at this moment.

Everything went against my expectations, I was asking myself Why we came, if we can struggle to have what we want and why we were starving ourselves. I asked my father if we should go back to village because I didn't see any difference from the way we lived in the village. He never Agreed and told me to wait.

"Everything is going to be okay, Don't worry Son! He said.

I dissolved in tears and never said a word. As you will see in the next chapter the situation was going from bad to worse and Suffering continued.

CHAPTER 3

LIVING IN POVERTY

What is poverty?

Poverty is about not having enough money to meet basic needs including food, clothing and shelter. However, poverty is more, much more than just not having enough money.

"Poverty is hunger. Poverty is lack of shelter. Poverty is being sick and not being able to see a doctor. Poverty is not having access to school and not knowing how to read. Poverty is not having a job, is fear for the future, living one day at a time.

Poverty has many faces, changing from place to place and across time, and has been described in many ways. Most often, poverty is a situation people want to escape. So poverty is a call to action – for the poor and the wealthy alike – a call to change the world so that many more may have enough to eat, adequate shelter, access to education and health, protection from violence, and a voice in what happens in their communities."

In addition to a lack of money, poverty is about not being able to participate in recreational activities; not being able to send children on a day trip with their schoolmates or to a birthday party; not being able to pay for medications for an illness. These are all costs of being poor. Those people who are barely able to pay for food and shelter simply can't consider these other expenses.

When people are excluded within a society, when they are not well educated and when they have a higher incidence of illness, there are negative consequences for society. We all pay the price for poverty. The increased cost on the health system, the justice system and other systems that provide supports to those living in poverty has an impact on our economy.

There is no one cause of poverty, and the results of it are different in every case. Poverty varies considerably depending on the situation. Feeling poor in Canada is different from living in poverty in Russia or Zimbabwe. The differences between rich and poor within the borders of a country can also be great.

Despite the many definitions, one thing is certain; poverty is a complex societal issue. No matter how poverty is defined, it can be agreed that it is an issue that requires everyone's attention. It is important that all members of our society work together to provide the opportunities for all our members to reach their full potential. It helps all of us to help one another.

Each nation may have its own criteria for determining the poverty line and counting how many of its people are living in poverty.

The impact of poverty on children is substantial. Children who grow up in poverty typically suffer from severe and frequent health problems; infants born into poverty have an increased chance of low birth weight, which can lead to physical and mental disabilities.

In some impoverished countries, poverty-stricken infants are nine times more likely to die in their first month compared to babies born in high-income countries.

Those who live may have hearing and vision problems.

Children in poverty tend to miss more school due to sickness and endure more stress at home. Homelessness is particularly hard on children because they often have little to no access to healthcare and lack proper nutrition—which often results in frequent health issues.

Homeless

  We had no home of our own. My father and I, still lived with Nick. And because we had no money, my father decided that we should start working for money by means of digging other people's farms.

We had no choice, and since we never had a house of our own, this was the only way we can survive. So the next day, we went out to look for a farm where we can work, and Luckily we found one.

However, we were not offered money to dig the farm. They offered us a single bread. We couldn't refuse because we needed money and we needed food too. So we had to dig a very big area for just bread and I was very tired, my father can testify.

We came back home (at Nick's house) and we shared the bread for supper.

The Next morning, I was starving, but still we had to go search for food just like we did on the previous day. I went with my Father and this day Nick came with us.

We found a place where we were offered money and we had to dig from 7am to 3pm. We got the money and we were all happy though it wasn't that enough.

When we reached home, we found no food was left for us. And the three of us had not eaten anything since morning. So I went to ask Grandma what we will eat.

" You won't eat Nothing! And if you have to eat, you should be eating only porridge once in a day. We have no food to waste." She said.

I didn't say a word, I just dissolved in tears and went to sleep. My father heard all that happened. So the next morning, he gave me some money to buy myself some food as I was starving for a day now.

I wonder the devil that told Grandma about my father giving me money for food. She never prepared anything for me when others were eating. And when I asked she said.

"Your father gave you money. Didn't you eat?" I looked at her and just turned went back out.

My father was hurt by all this, so when she realized my father was hurt, she made porridge for my supper and gave it to me.

Sometimes we were eating porridge only for the all day and sometimes starving the all day or two.

Life was hard and my hopes for the future vanished, my hopes for school crushed. And I couldn't think of any positive thing this time. I never wanted to ask my father about school, for I knew he was already going through a lot.

A month later

We were given a potion of two hectors to cultivate our own food.

"We should cultivate maize and Sell them for profit." My father said.

" Yes Dad." I agreed.

After this conversation with him, I was strengthened and I could vision myself moving to our own house. We began to dig our own land a few days later.

We did it all by ourselves, "Yes just him and I." We planted maize and grew it so well.

After harvesting, things started to get a bit better. But we were still at Nick's house. So my father told me that he will find a house soon and we will start living on our own. I was very happy to hear this.

My father found a friend. His friend had some experience in construction. So they thought and planed to start building house's for people.

When my father told me he is opening a construction company with a friend, I was very excited.

"Can you open a company without finishing school?" I asked.

"Yes You can. And you can also be a business Man without school my Son." He said.

I was very surprised because I never heard this from anyone. I never believed him, because my grandpa and my teacher told me that school is the only way to achieving anything.

How to escape poverty
- **Stop being Entitled**

It's not circumstances that keep us where we are; it is what we think and say about ourselves. But seeing yourself as deserving success is one thing; getting other people to see you that way is another. You may feel you deserve to be handed a job because you spent five years of hard work studying at the university. But for other people, you are just another millennial that has a lot to learn.

You may think you deserve special treatment because you have suffered abuse and extreme poverty in the past; but most people are too busy dealing with their own problem.

- **People only respect previous results.**

That is why success continues to beget more success. If you are searching on "How to build a parachute" online and two videos show up; one has 415 views, the other has 1.5 million views, which are you going to choose? That's it. You'll choose the more successful one. It is why Samsung phones and iPhone continues to outsell the new phone companies. People unconsciously value sacrifice and result. They expect you to pay your dues.

If you haven't done anything worthy of accolades, and you go about making demands, you are just being entitled. Get to work building your profile. Go out and start doing that thing you believe is beneath you. Learn that handiwork. Take up that job you believe is below your qualification. No one is going to lay that foundation for you; you have to do it yourself.

- **Remove Yourself from the statistic of the Poor.**

The first step to help the poor is to not be one of the poor. With the limitless knowledge and resources available today, it will be too selfish of you to remain poor. Here is why.

By using the resources within your disposal to get out of poverty, you mathematically reduce the number of poor people in the world, not just by one but by many. That knowledge; that idea; that skill you have, can help take care of two, three or more people. It will be unfair if you don't develop it.

Another important reason to remove yourself from the poor is that – If you want to get what you don't have, you have to do what you have never done. Poverty comes with a lot of mental baggage. You can't become a person of success while still identifying yourself as poor. Eliminate all those labels associated with poverty from your lips. Stop referring yourself as among "the poor masses". Start surrounding yourself with progressive people.

- **Stop caring what other people think**

Little minded people are like crabs. You've probably heard about crabs, haven't you? If you put, let's say 47 crabs inside a bucket without covering the lead, none of them will be able to get out. In reality, they could simply climb on each other and find their way out; but not these creatures. They will rather pull down anyone of them that tries to find their way out. In their mind, "we all die here". Little minds who don't have the courage to work themselves out of their below average life, are often fond of talking down on people who want to try. These people will rarely support or patronize what you offer. But they'll be the first to tell you why this is not for you.

If your strategy in life is to end up pleasing everyone, you will end up miserable; trapped in the same mess. So, you must train yourself to ignore crab minded people. Let them keep their opinion while you keep your dream alive.

- **Start seeing 'yourself' in Successful people**

We are all humans; and we have the natural tendencies to be selfish. Even religions depend on "What's in it for the convert" like eternal life and prosperity. Poor people see these attribute of selfishness as belonging to the rich, so they portray this false humility to mask their true desire. The truth is that you can't become what you hate. If you continue to see progressive people as antagonists, you'll never understand what it'll take to make progress.

No doubt, some people take their greed and selfishness to the extreme and only live to oppress other people. But the magic is to understand this inherent human nature, that everyone you meet is first and foremost more interest in "what's in it for them". People are always thinking about themselves. With this knowledge, start focusing more on what people want and what you can offer them. "You can have all you want in life if you can help as much people get what they want". Turn the focus of your life towards identifying and providing what other people want and you will be on your way to getting what you want.

- Learn a skill and get good at it

On a deeper level, the problem of poverty is not lack of money but lack of skill. The best strategy to escape poverty is to learn a skill people want to pay for. Interestingly, there is an avalanche of free resources to help you develop and brush up your skills; from programming, design to marketing skills. There is also carpentry, shoe making, car mechanic and other handwork. This is where you need to keep your entitlement mindset to check. As long as you are doing decent work, and earning a living off it, you should be confident and proud of what you do.

- Move your service from intermediate to professional

Listen attentively to this. People do not hire you or patronize your business or service because they want to help you get out of poverty. They do so because they need to solve a problem. Many people get trapped in the circle of poverty and mediocrity by offering poor and nonchalant services. They go about their work like hunting; every encounter is hunt and kill. They leave each prospect bitter and vowing never to patronize them again.

Don't toll this path. Instead, keep in mind that people are inherently selfish; they want to be treated well; they want good result. Focus on helping them get what they want, so that you can get what you want. Instead of treating your work as hunting, decide to treat it as gardening. If you are in business, you need repeat patronage; in the professional world, you need referrals and recommendations. Don't go about burning your bridges. Start cultivating positive relationships around your work.

- Learn to sell

What do you think is the highest paid profession in the world? It's not medical doctors or engineers. The highest paid profession in the world is sales. The richest people are the best at selling; whether it's selling their vision, their product and service or their skills. They are masters at selling.

The ability to sell is not reserved for a few set of people. Anyone can learn this skill. The problem is that most people spend too much time on the product and too little on selling what they have. If you want to escape poverty, the ability to sell can get you out faster than any other skill. There is no best-written author, but best-selling author.

- Take Back Control of Your mind

Most of your opinions are not original. They were adopted from your environment into your mind. Each time you turn on the TV, go on social media, listen to people around, your mind is getting suggestions on opinions to hold or to let go.

Here is an example. Do you know that mega supermarkets are designed to make you buy more than what you had in mind to buy? You walk in to get a deal on one item and you walk out buying a cart full of items; some of which you don't need. How would you explain that almost everyone in Africa seems to fanatically support a football club in England or Spain? Or that millions of people lost their money in a Ponzi scheme that promised 30 percent interest every month.

If you take the time to ponder, you will realize that you are not as in control of your mind as you think. You will realize that some of the things you spend time, energy and money on are actually not worth much. Your mind is your most valuable asset. Take back control of it by deciding what you let into it. Read books and stories that inspire you to dream and take productive action. Invest in yourself. I learned all this when I saw my father doing something about our poverty situation.

This moment, My father did something to escape poverty, he used his skills to open a construction company. And after a month we moved to our own house. But still life was hard for me, Because I was supposed to remain home all by myself, Cook for myself as well as cooking for my father.

We had no Bed or mattress, so we could sleep on the floor. Nevertheless I was happy this way because I wasn't starving no more like I used to be.

However, my Dream of being a pilot, was shutting down everyday. I was growing and I couldn't start school in grade 1 cause there were only kids and am a bit older than them. So embarrassing you know.

After 4 Years of living with my Father and establishing a living, he decided that everyone should now come from the village and live with us. Our house was also in a village like compound. We were not living in town, but village.

18th November 2012 my family came. I was very happy to see my mother again and everyone else. But to my mother this was so surprising because she thought she will come to a very big house and beautiful home town. Guess what she found, Another village. She was happy still though it's not what she expected.

After three (3) months, something so brilliant happened. It was heart relieving.

"We will be going to school tomorrow and talk to the headteacher so you can resume school again." My mother said.

"WOW. Are you serious?" I replied.

"Yes, we will." She concluded.

I was so happy the all day. My face couldn't lose a smile. I used to laugh even when something isn't funny, because of the happiness I felt inside. "I will now be a pilot." Saying from the heart.

The next day my mother went to school, but to the sad part she had no transfer later to take to the headmaster for my school clarifications. So he refused to hear her and told her to come with me the next day.

We went there and he began to ask me very tough questions. I answered some of his questions, and to his analysis, he decided that I should go direct to grade 6. With that said, I never attended grade 2, 3, 4 and 5th Grade.

I started in grade 6 and at this time they were already in the last term of grade 6. Only one year we will be writing the Exams, it was hard to catch up and I didn't know where to start from.

The Headteacher called me to his office, I thought he will tell me to stop going to school at this point. I entered his Office.

"Take a sit Son." He said.

I sat down and waited for him to speak.

"Are You ready for the Exams?" He asked.

"I don't know if I'm ready Sir, because this is my second day in school and I don't know what to study, where to start from and how it should be done. I don't even know the arrangements for the Exams." I replied.

"Well, if you were given where to start from and what to study, how best can you do it and how much time are you ready to invest?" He asked.

"I want to Learn how to be a pilot, I want to fly a plane, so I'm ready to invest all of my time in it." I said.

He laughed, and just gave me 5 books.

"Read them and prepare for your Exams. You'll write Exams next Year." He said.

I left his Office with smiles on my face. I still never had a bag, so I got the Books he gave me and put them in my plastic bag. I went back home, showed Mom and Dad the books and explained what happened.

I couldn't sleep that Night, I finished the all candle just reading one of the Books I was Given. I didn't understand anything, but I still continued to read, I was just mastering instead of understanding what I couldn't.

I didn't find the chapter I was looking for, I wanted to read about airplanes and how to fly them, but I never found this chapter. So the next day I went to my Headteacher for he is the One who gave me books.

"I didn't find a chapter of being a pilot in the books you gave me, can you give me that Book sir?" I said.

Smiling, he said: " I would like you to focus on the same books for now for they are a way to get you where you want to be." I don't know how to fly a plane and I can't teacher you that, but if you focus, You will learn that soon." He said.

I went back and studied the Books, though it's not everything I understood, I was mastering and memorizing the points to help me answer questions. The information were a bit confusing and puzzling. But I still managed to read the all five Books as I was so interested in reading books.

We wrote the Exams and I made it, I even got better than some of those who attended all levels of school before the 7th grade.

CHAPTER 4

ESCAPING POVERTY

In economics, a cycle of poverty or poverty trap is caused by self-reinforcing mechanisms that cause poverty, once it exists, to persist unless there is outside intervention.

It can persist across generations, and when applied to developing countries, is also known as a development trap.

Families trapped in the cycle of poverty have few to no resources. There are many self-reinforcing disadvantages that make it virtually impossible for individuals to break the cycle.

This occurs when poor people do not have the resources necessary to escape poverty, such as financial capital, education, or connections. Impoverished individuals do not have access to economic and social resources as a result of their poverty. This lack may increase their poverty. This could mean that the poor remain poor throughout their lives.

In chapter 5 of the Book: **THE WALK TO FINANCIAL FREEDOM,** I've distinguished between situational poverty, which can generally be traced to a specific incident within the lifetimes of the person or family members in poverty, and generational poverty, which is a cycle that passes from generation to generation, and goes on to argue that generational poverty has its own distinct culture and belief patterns. You can find the book on Amazon.com

My father worked really hard to get something done for the family and to just escape the poverty level. He decided that we should find a house in town and leave the village.

Two weeks later he found a house and we moved to town. It was so good because I could now live in a place where I'll see electricity everyday. He bought a TV, I could watch TV now.

However, I couldn't go to school now because of some financial issues as we were still struggling to find a good life. They couldn't take me to High school due to Money issues. So, I stayed in the village when my friends were doing the 8th Grade.

I forgot everything I learned in school, I really wanted to learn how to be a pilot. I'm sure if I learned that subject in the books I was given, I wouldn't have forgotten.

After 3 Years of staying in the village, they took me back to school, so I can resume. I was happy and couldn't wait to study a subject about being a pilot or how to fly an airplane.

They got a Transfer, but when they went to my former Headteacher, he decided to take me direct to grade 9. And he wrote a letter saying I should start grade 9.

Only two Months remained to sign in for Exams. This is real story, I was shocked when they Enrolled me because I was only having a shot time to study and prepare for my Exams. Unlike grade 6, I didn't have the all year to study and prepare, I only had a Few months. But similarly to the 6th Grade, I was given books to study. And I took Agriculture Science too.

I studied what I never understood, even now I can't remember everything I was studying, but luckily I made it and I got better grades. Even this time, No one could teach me How to fly an airplane and being a good pilot. I was sent to study courses that I couldn't remember until I learned how to memorize the information.

I started my 10th Grade at LUBUTO SECONDARY SCHOOL in Ndola Zambia. It was awesome because you know, I thought this grade had a subject for pilots.

"You should Focus on this School, as it is your last chance of getting the job you want. Get Good grades so that you can find a Better Job." My class teacher said.

"Sir. I have a question." I said.

"Go ahead." He replied.

"Will I be employed as a pilot after getting Good grades in this school?" I asked.

"Not right after you get good grades, you'll have to go to college spend years in college and get a PHD, masters or degree for that course, then you'll be employed as a pilot." He said.

This was not okay with me, as it seemed to be a way of consuming my all time and life to get a life I wanted to live. I was disturbed after hearing this, and I began to think if there was a shortcut I would have taken to get me where I wanted.

"Why didn't I start with college then, because I never needed all the things I studied, things I couldn't even remember. Why didn't they take me direct to study a course I wanted. This is a wrong and longcut." Thinking to myself.

I continued to study so I can find what I need. I used to Go to school in the morning around 7am and come back home at night, around 6pm, just studying the Books.

Because of the life I lived and how I struggled in my earliest stage of life, I never wanted to suffer or to be poor I may say. I was looking for a way to financial freedom, I really needed a path I should take, a shortcut to success than going through the all process's I was told to go through by my teacher.

I couldn't rest, I used to read so many books only searching for a way to financial freedom.

When I was in the 11th grade, I stopped focusing on school, because I never found the subject I was looking for. From the 1st grade to the 11th, I never found what I needed.

Throughout my research, I came across the Book, Rich Dad, Poor Dad, by Robert Kiyosaki. And the Book, THINK AND GROW RICH. These two books changed my vision and I completely stopped studying school books. I focused on understanding these books. I was able to understand everything and I was now able to differentiate between Rich and Poor people.

I realized the way I should have gone and I regretted not knowing all the information when I was starting to discover myself in my early childhood, I felt like I wasted too much time.

After a couple of days at school, my teacher said the same thing he said the other day. " Focus or else you'll be poor without school." He said.

"No. that is a lie, there are better ways to do with life than even school." I said.

"Are you saying you know better than I do?" He rudely asked, called me to the front to explain myself to the pupils on what I was talking about. Pupils laughed at me and it was a bit annoying.

"Tell us what you're talking about." He said.

I began to explain what I learned in just one year, and I said:

So you want to get a Degree? Why? Let me tell you what society will tell you. "Education (which is school in most cases) increases your chances of getting a job, provides you with even opportunity to be successful, your life will be a lot less stressful **Education is the Key** ".

Now let me tell you what your parents will tell you. " Make me proud. Education increases your chances of getting a job provides you with even opportunity of being successful your life will be a lot less stressful **Education is the Key** ".

Now Let's Look at the statistics.

Steve Jobs: Networth 9 Billion

Richard Branson: Networth 6.2 Billion

Oprah Winfrey: Networth 4.3 Billion.

Looking at these Individuals, what's your conclusion? Neither of them has been Successful after Graduating from a higher Learning institution.

Now some of you will protest like, "You know money is a medium by which someone measures the worldly Success". And some of you even have the nerve to say " I don't do it for the money". Then what are you studying for? Is it to work for a charity or You need more clarity? Let's look at the statistics.

- **Jesus**
- **Muhammad Feals**
- **Muhammad Harry**
- **Shown Coah**
- **Michael Joffrey Jordan**
- **Michael Joseph Jackson.**

Who ever of these people were successful but uneducated. All am saying is, if there was a family tree, hard work and education will be related, but school can only be a district cousin, Because if Education is the key then school is the lock. It makes the mindset developed the Program of saying Red is Green, and Green is Red.

This Program developed makes a person to continue going even when someone has said stop. Because as long as you follow the rules and pass Exams, then you are cool, but are you aware that Examiners has a checklist?

They say school expands your vision and chances. Tell that to Michael Matteson who dropped out of school and was well announced for what he learned in prison.

Proverbs 17:16; "It does a fool to spend money on Education. Why? Because he has no conscience."

Education is about inspiring someone's Mind not just feeding their head. And take this from me because am an educated mind by myself.

I only came to this realization after countless nights in the library of a Kind where you read books that keeps you Awake. I was falling asleep in between the purse of books which probably equates to the Same amount of time I spent memorizing equations, facts and dates half of which I never remember and half of which I forgot right after the stop of the next semester.

I often found myself running in the class, just so I can find this book where I can rest my head without making a sin. I've been running all the time I've spent in basic and high school just Chasing my Dreams.

Now am not saying school is bad and there's nothing to gain. All am saying is understand your motives and reassess your Ends. Because if you want a job working for someone else, then help yourself. Then that will be a contradiction because you wouldn't really be helping yourself if you work for someone, as a saying which says; "If you don't build your dreams someone else will hire you to build their's.." Redefine how you view Education, understand its true meaning.

Education is not just about regards to read the fractional books and someone else's opinion or Subject to pass an Exam. Pecasal was Educated in creating arts. Michael Matteson was Educated in prison. Understand what the value of Education is Redefine it and Build yourself Based on what works not what doesn't.

Everyone was surprised to hear me speak like this.

"Where did you Learn that?" my teacher asked.

"I needed to learn how to be a pilot since my childhood, this is why I needed school, from the start of my education up to today, I never learned about what I needed, no one taught me what I want. So, I began a new journey of searching for financial freedom and found books like I mentioned, that satisfied my need." I said.

My teacher went away without saying a word and to everyone who laughed at me, I gained respect. This is how my life began changing. I began the Walk to Financial Freedom.

What is Financial Freedom

Attaining financial freedom is an objective for most individuals. Financial freedom usually means having enough savings, financial investments, and cash on hand to afford the kind of life we desire for ourselves and our families. It means growing savings that enable us to retire or pursue the career we want without being driven by earning a set salary each year. Financial freedom means our money is working for us rather than the other way around.

To become financially free, you must pay off your consumer debts, build a safety net of savings funds, and create enough passive income through investing or business ownership to pay for your current and expected future living expenses.

We are burdened with increasing debt, monetary emergencies, excessive consumer spending, and other problems that keep us from reaching our most meaningful financial objectives, Such challenges confront everybody.

Financial freedom means you have enough financial resources to pay for your living expenses and allow you to afford many of your life goals without having to work or otherwise commit any of your time or efforts to generating money.

When you have financial freedom, you control your money instead of letting it control you. As a result, you often experience less stress and have more time to do the things you love. If financial freedom is a goal you want to reach, figuring out how it works and how much money you need to reach it is a great place to start.

By having financial freedom, you can make decisions that align with your values and life goals instead of worrying about how you'll make your next paycheck.

Financial freedom and well-being can further be defined through these four elements:

1. Having control over your day-to-day, and month-to-month finances
2. Having the ability to absorb financial shock
3. Being on track to meet your financial goals
4. Making the choices that enable you to best enjoy life.

How Does Financial Freedom Work?

The process of working toward financial freedom can be broken down into a few key steps.

Define what financial freedom means to you: If you had all the money in the world, how would you spend your days? What would you want to accomplish in life?

Figure out how much money you need to afford your version of financial freedom: Calculate how much money you need to save in order to fund the lifestyle outlined in the previous step. How much money you'll need to have saved depends on your expected annual expenses.

Save as much as you can: When you reach financial freedom, you are no longer living paycheck to paycheck, but instead have enough funds to last and protect you in the event of an emergency. By continuing to save as much as you can, you will be one step closer to your savings goals, no matter what those may be.

Live below your means and save the rest: If you are able to, spending less than you earn is recommended for reaching financial freedom.

How Much Money Do I Need to Reach Financial Freedom?

As mentioned, there is no one amount of money that every person should reach for in order to achieve financial freedom. The amount will vary depending on the individual and their lifestyle goals.

Generally, though, the amount of money you need to reach financial freedom depends on your expected annual expenses, as well as your annual income. The multiply-by-30 rule is a helpful guide individuals use to calculate how much they should save for retirement, and it can be applied to financial freedom, as well:

Financial freedom (quantity) = expected annual income x 30

Let's say you need to have $50,000 a year to afford your dream lifestyle. In this case, your financial freedom amount would be somewhere $1.25 million just to estimate.

Ideally, though, in addition to saving regularly from your salary, you would increase the amount of money you save through things like 401(k) employer matches, compound interest on investments, and other sources of passive income.

Financial Freedom is a term that we often come across nowadays. Different people come up with different definitions. Some say: It's about buying what you want and when you want; having no debt; being able to support yourself, or simply being rich.

Well, these are just vague and half-baked answers. Though we often spend time discussing the topic and how we can achieve financial freedom, the truth is we are completely clueless about what it actually means.

And, if we don't have a clear idea about what our goal is, how can we ever reach there. Financial Freedom is not about being rich and having tons of money, but having enough to cover your expenses so that you can spend your precious time doing what you like rather than doing things just to earn money. This can be achieved only when you are prepared for it. All you need is a little financial planning.

How to Achieve Financial Freedom

- Understand Current Financial Conditions

The first step in achieving financial freedom is knowing your financial condition. How much is the fixed income and the amount of routine expenses each month, and whether there is a debt or not? If the obligations you have to pay each month are greater than your monthly income, then you have not yet reached the concept of financial freedom.

Determine in the future, whether you want to reduce the obligation that comes from debt, or even increase the amount of income. By knowing your current financial conditions and needs, you will be more focused on achieving future financial goals.

- Do Financial Planning Carefully

The next step is to do careful financial planning. The need to apply the right way of managing finances, determining how long a person's financial freedom can be achieved. You must be able to allocate each expense item wisely. For example, what percentage is allocated to finance daily expenses, what percentage is for savings and emergency funds, and what percentage is to pay installments if any?

Every individual's financial planning is different, but maybe you can use the 4-3-2-1 method as a reference. That is, allocate 40% of your total income per month to finance daily expenses such as food, transportation, electricity, internet, and others. Then, allocate 30% to pay installments or debts if any. Always try to pay debts on time so you don't get fined and have a good credit score. Next, allocate 20% to saving and setting up an emergency fund. The remaining 10% is allocated to do good activities such as charity or alms.

- Have Sufficient Savings

Having sufficient savings is very important to achieve the concept of financial freedom because these funds will be very useful in the future. You can take advantage of the auto-debit feature from your bank so that it is always routine to save every month. For the amount, you can refer to the formula for setting the 4-3-2-1 salary that has been mentioned above. Allocating more than 20% every month for savings, of course, is better, as long as your daily needs can be met.

Set a saving goal to prepare for a more mature future such as funding children's education costs, renovating a house, buying priority items, or other positive activities.

- Looking for Additional Income by Doing Business

If you have more time and energy, it never hurts to get additional income from various sources. For example, you can run a side business that doesn't interfere with your main job. There are many types of side businesses that you can run. Start with a small side business first.

If your business has grown and would need additional funds as business capital, you can apply for a business capital loan from a Financial Service Provider. A business capital loan, it does not necessarily discourage you from achieving the concept of financial freedom. As long as you can manage your business well and pay your loan installments on time, your goal of financial freedom can still be achieved.

- Invest

To achieve financial freedom, you should also make investments that are tailored to your risk profile. If you are a beginner in this investment activity, try investing with low risks such as mutual funds or gold. The investment aims to develop assets either in real or visible and financial investments. So, the benefits will be felt in the next few years.

- Pay Off Debt on Time

Debt is okay as long as you are fully responsible for returning it according to the agreed nominal value. Having accumulated debt will certainly make life feel more difficult and far from this financial freedom terminology. So, before you go into debt, set a clear goal for what you owe and adjust it to your financial condition.

Paying debts on time will maintain the quality of good relations between parties. In addition, if you pay debts on time to Financial Institutions, it will save you from a bad credit score and pending late payment penalties.

- Prepare an Emergency Fund

It should be emphasized again, that the concepts of emergency funds and savings are different. Although both are funds that are set aside from the income we receive each month, they both have different goals. Emergency funds are funds that are kept to finance uncertain conditions when and for what use. In other words, emergency funds are used to finance unforeseen conditions such as if there is a family who becomes suddenly ill, finances daily expenses in case of termination of employment (PHK), and so on.

Meanwhile, savings funds are funds that are kept to finance conditions that have been clearly defined in advance. Such as savings for weddings, savings for education, savings for home renovations, and others.

There is no definite formula for the size of the emergency fund. However, you can refer to the amount 6 times your monthly expenses. No less important, separate your emergency fund account from your daily savings and expense account, so you are not tempted to use the collected emergency funds.

- Adopt a Simple Lifestyle

The final step in achieving the concept of financial freedom is to adopt a simple lifestyle. Don't be influenced to live beyond your means or hedonic. In addition to quickly depleting funds, either from savings or your regular income, a hedonic lifestyle will trigger unnecessary debt.

A simple lifestyle can be started by diligently saving, shopping sparingly, and avoiding debt if you can't pay it off.

- Coming up with Something

You can build or create something that people would love to buy forever and generate residual income from it. You can write books, building Website, making a company and many more. In the next chapter I'll Talk about how I began my journey to financial freedom.

Well, that's how to achieve complete financial freedom. To achieve it is not easy, it takes high consistency and hard effort.

CHAPTER 5

JOURNEY TO FINANCIAL FREEDOM

During my search for financial freedom, I continued to discover many things about success, I could read books that was changing my thinking and abilities to take action on my financial Growth.

Being a pilot was my goal when I was a kid. So, when I discovered it was almost impossible for me due to the life I lived, my goal changed and I discovered my career.

One important secret to success and Financial freedom is to discover your career and work on it. I discovered my career, because I realized it wasn't easy for me to be a pilot. My parents had no enough money to pay for my college education, I couldn't pay for myself the all years am supposed to be in college. Unless if I started when I was a Kid learning this skill, by this time I would have made it and Learnt the all process and mostly how to fly a plane.

After a few months of research, I found that I can do a lot of things that don't even need a college degree to become Financially Stable and Free. There are thousands of people who never went to school, dropped out of school and became successful.

Steve Jobs, the founder of Apple, dropped out of college at 19, but he Built Apple Company and became successful.

Bill Gates dropped out of Harvard after two years, built Microsoft and became successful.

Evan Williams, the founder of Twitter, attended college for three semesters before dropping out. Built Twitter and became successful.

Mark Zuckerberg dropped out of Harvard and said it took him 5 minutes to make that decision. Built Facebook and become successful.

I'm not saying that you should drop out of college or School. I think school and any higher Learning institution is fantastic. But I just don't think it's always necessary for someone to Achieve Financial Freedom.

These are things I found during my research and it helped me to start thinking of building something that will benefit others, and this thing must make me successful too.

In August 2017, I started writing my first Book, THE WALK TO FINANCIAL FREEDOM. In this book I've outlined everything a person must do to help him/her self to build the life that leads to success and even financial freedom. You can find it on Amazon: author Leonard Mukuka

I couldn't focus on school no more, because what I found made me change the decision and dreams I had. "I don't want to be a pilot no more. I want to be Financially free." I kept saying to myself. I stayed focused on writing the book.

We wrote the Exams and though I got Few things right, I got less than my parents expected, they were shocked.

"Why have you failed? You were doing better but why have you brought this shame upon yourself? How will you live a good life with these zeros?" they said.

I couldn't answer them and as I never wanted to tell them the reason and what I was thinking.

"How will you be a pilot?" Dad asked.

"I don't want to be a pilot no more. There's so much time to be wasted for me to reach there and I might grow old poor." I said.

They never understood what I was talking about, for they knew that school is the secret to success, which was not true for me according to what I discovered at this time.

I continued with writing and it took me 3 years to finish writing my first book. I never had the money to publish the book so I thought I should find some money so that I can publish the book and teach my entrepreneurship ideas to people around the world and at the same time generate income.

What is a Career?

What is the meaning of 'Career'; this is often a question that lurks in the minds of students. A career is an individual's 'journey' of lifelong learning, working, extensive training and learning new skills.

It can be described as an employment or a vocation that generally involves some specialized training or formal study. In simple terms, a career is what you do for a living. As you gain more experience in life and in work, you are building your career. There are numerous ways to define what is a career

The Oxford English Dictionary defines the word "career" as a person's "course or progress through life (or a distinct portion of life)". The word 'career' is also used to refer to an occupation, profession, vocation or employment. The career path that you follow takes into account your education.

Training, jobs that you get paid for or any volunteer work. For example – A career could mean working as a Doctor , Lawyer , Engineer , etc. This broadly explains what is the meaning of 'career'. Let us now know more about what is a career.

To understand what the meaning of a 'career' is, it is essential to understand the difference between job and career.

A job is a work activity that you take up and get paid for those certain tasks you perform. A job can be full-time or part-time, or even for a short term. You might need to learn specialized skills connected with that job role, but not all jobs require specialized training.

Let's say, a company hires a local building contractor to complete an office renovation. The company and the contractor agree upon the terms of payment duration , so the job ends once the project is finished and the office is renovated.

However, a career might last for your entire life. It consists of all the jobs you have done in your chosen industry and progressed through during your career, regardless of whether or not they are associated with each other.

- What is a career goal?

Once we have understood what is the meaning of a 'career', we can move on to know what is a career goal. Any long term professional path you may plan for yourself, based on your interests and ambitions will be your career goal. They are professional targets that you set your mind on achieving.

They can be short term, for e.g. getting admission in a particular college for a particular course, or they can be long term, for e.g. like being a CEO at your dream company.

Understanding what is a career goal and formulating one for yourself can help you select the right courses and work on developing the right skills.

- What is a career plan?

Since we now have clarity on what is the meaning of a 'career', and what is a career goal, let us understand what is a career plan. A career plan includes interim goals, eventual career goals, and all the efforts you make to achieve them.

For Example: Understanding what is a career plan and creating one for yourself can help you decide what subjects to choose in class 11, what extracurricular activities you should take part in, or which internships will help you become a strong job candidate and other words, which can help you become Financially Free.

It is also important to be practical about your career goals and timelines. Career action plans can help you achieve your goals and stay organized.

Students often face the dilemma of 'What career should I choose?'. Understanding the different types of career pathways might help you formulate an idea of what type of a career you would want. A career path is a particular sequence of jobs that helps you progress towards your career goals. Different types of career pathways can be:-

1. *Discovering your niche*

Your career comprises numerous jobs that are entirely unrelated to one another. It is a chance to explore all the available options. Working on different jobs might help you understand better what might be the best fit for you.

For Example: You start with an internship at a fashion design studio, and you might be studying business management, and then you might start working with any of the BIG 4 companies after finishing your graduation. Or Building something of your own, based on your studies.

2. *Advancing in the same profession*

The second path involves advancing in the same occupation, with a series of higher positions and responsibilities that are interconnected to each other. You might be working for the same organization or at different companies.

For Example: If you want to be an Educationist or Principal of a school, you will start with working as a teacher, then can move to a different role of being a curriculum coordinator, to the vice-principal and after gaining a few years of experience, you may become the Principal of a school.

3. *Moving up the ladder through different roles, but same industry*

This path involves moving up the higher positions professionally through diversified roles in the same industry, but does not mean that you work in the same occupation.

Your ultimate goal in life is to be a retail chain store manager, you can begin doing an internship at a retail chain store, then qualify for a salesperson position. After gaining some experience you may become a department manager, then assistant store manager, store manager, and Eventually the CEO of your own Store.

Financial Freedom is a process. It doesn't happen overnight, be ready to put in the work and much effort to achieve everything you need.

Months Later

I started searching for a job so I can make the money to publish my book and get it the world, I didn't find a job, for Jobs are not easily found in my country (Zambia).

I decided that I should join my father in his construction company, work with him and he pays me.

"I want to work with you, I want to learn construction from you?" I said telling my father.

"Are you strong enough for it?" He asked.

"Yes. I can work, so long as am paid." I said, for my aim was only to hunt for money so that I can continue on the journey of publishing the book.

"Okay, You'll start next week." He said.

After a week of working for him. He paid us. The money wasn't enough compared to the Job we were doing. Construction is a hard job if you're not the Boss, but just a worker.

I could work the all day under the Sun and only eat less for Lunch. I was getting the money but it wasn't enough to help me with what I needed. I used to find that, the all money is finished before the next payment, just trying to take care of myself and the little things like clothing's.

I had no much in my servings account, I continued to work and I started loosing focus on my goals and Vision.

How to stay Focused

Most people fail not because they lack the ability or resources. It's simply because they lose focus.

"Successful people understand that without focus one cannot take the necessary steps to create a vision." The successful warrior is the average man, with laser-like focus."

We all know and Understand that, staying focused is more and more difficult in the modern world. Yes, the demands of our daily work, with constantly incoming emails and texts, meetings, conference calls and video chat with contacts near and far, the need to keep up with social media, as well as the avalanche of important news about whatever industry you're in all encourage us or force us—to rapidly move our attention from one thing to another during the course of our workdays, and the days we are off.

There is only one problem. The more we pay attention to these things, the less we are able to focus. "Because the brain gets good at whatever it practices, when you lose focus, you eventually train your brain for distraction." With that said the power to create vision, is lost in the process." "Distraction is a death sentence for manifesting one's vision."

No matter what you vision, you won't be able to move toward it if you only feel anxiety, anger, frustration, hopelessness, shame, guilt, or jealousy. There's no outcome to create from such lower emotional patterns.

On the other hand, if you feel peace, love, joy, gratitude, or compassion, you eventually gain the traits to achieving your vision. Use the skills you learn in meditation to move your emotional state from one State to the other.

Ask yourself this one question, 'What takes me closer to my vision?' If a choice takes you closer to your vision, then follow that path. "If it takes you away from realizing your intended creation, then go in the other direction."

Having a vision doesn't always mean that you know exactly how to get there. It's about having a clear idea of where you want to reach and end up, not actually every step along the way. "Focus on embodying the mental, emotional, and physical state, and take action from that state. When you get distracted, "Slowly direct your focus back to the vision you have chosen."

Working from an emotional place of peace, love, and gratitude is so valuable. Only when you can do that. "You can rest assured that you are aligned with your vision and on the path to achieving it."

Becoming A Successful Entrepreneur

It's important to understand that there is no magic bullet that can transform you into a rich and successful entrepreneur overnight. However, for those prepared to work hard to succeed, there is an almost formulaic blend of entrepreneurial skills that can help set successful businessmen and women.

Becoming a successful entrepreneur doesn't just happen overnight; but you'll find the following characteristics are typical in the majority of successful business people that have navigated their way to the top:

- Never take 'No' for an answer

No matter how many knock-backs and refusals successful entrepreneurs receive, they are always prepared to dust themselves down and find an alternative route to the summit. It's this kind of tenacity which is required to take a business idea from the realms of the mind and transform it into a profitable business.

Fear of failure is one reason that many entrepreneurs fall by the wayside. Successful entrepreneurs view failure as a positive experience – something to learn from and overcome in the future. All entrepreneurs inevitably make mistakes along the path to success. But what matters most is that you own your failures and take full responsibility for the knock-backs and move forward quickly.

- Learn from the best

Even the very best entrepreneurs of our time worked with other experts in their industry before going it alone. Finding a suitable mentor is a great way to learn more about your sector as a whole and, more importantly, the various facets of running your very own business. Your mentor may even have made mistakes in business themselves, but equally that makes them the perfect person to learn from, giving you the chance to understand where they went wrong.

- Stay hungry and ambitious

Running a successful business is not an ego trip for successful entrepreneurs. It's their desire to grow and provide a better product or service for their customers that keeps them hungry and ambitious. The moment that an entrepreneur stops wanting to learn new things is the moment that complacency sets in, allowing others to overtake you and leave you behind. Which leads us nicely into…

- Never stand still; evolve with the times

Any successful entrepreneur requires business agility, with the ability to learn and adapt to new methods, processes or technology that can make their business stronger and more efficient. Market needs have always been dynamic: both the business and consumer worlds are ever-changing and what worked years, even months ago might not work tomorrow.

Successful entrepreneurs are never too proud to accept when there are new opportunities to enhance their offering and better satisfy the needs of their customers and the market as a whole. A product developed strictly for your own needs would be classed more like a hobby; however, a product developed for the market must be designed to satisfy evolving market needs.

- Nurture long-term business relationships

There are no two ways about it, business relationships matter. Almost always businesses will prefer to work with companies they like and trust. Your ability to nurture long-term working relationships with like-minded entrepreneurs within your industry will be one of the key factors in the long-term success of the business. Most entrepreneurs would agree it's far easier to secure work from repeat customers than it is investing time and money into securing new customers.

Business relationships also include access to finance too. Every entrepreneur wants the very best opportunity to see their business proposition become an established company. This means entrepreneurs have to become highly investable. By nurturing relationships with angel and seed investors, venture capitalists, private investors and even banks, you can set the wheels in motion to secure that all-important entrepreneur funding.

- Inspire those around you

Even the richest, most experienced entrepreneurs cannot be good at everything! All entrepreneurs require a team of people around them that complement their skills. The real skill is not only hiring the best possible team to support you, it's about hiring people who share your vision and passion. By inspiring and investing in your team, not only will they succeed but the business itself will too.

Success is the state or condition of meeting a defined range of expectations. It may be viewed as the opposite of failure. The criteria for success depend on context, and may be relative to a particular observer or belief system. One person might consider a success what another person considers a failure, particularly in cases of direct competition or a zero-sum game. Similarly, the degree of success or failure in a situation may be differently viewed by distinct observers or participants, such that a situation that one considers to be a success, another might consider to be a failure, a qualified success or a neutral situation.

Truth About Financial Freedom

The lie: A college degree guarantees a high-paying job.

While many degree programs do in fact pave the way to a six-figure career, getting a diploma does not mean you will earn six figures. When you see the amount of degree holders that remain underemployed and underpaid, it's clear a degree isn't a guarantee of a great career.

Am not saying college degrees are useless and there's nothing to gain or that you shouldn't attend a four-year institution — just that they aren't required to achieve success.

The issue with the equation "School (college) is a key to success," is that a formal, academic education is not for everyone.

Talent and marketable skills can make you successful, even without a college Degree.

Look at the construction industry. Careers in carpentry, electrical, ironwork or pipefitting require only a high school diploma to get started because skilled professionals in these crafts can learn on the job and through specialized craft training.

One of the essential things that school does not teach us is financial education. Money handling or money managing is another essential part of our lives to build our wealth. There are so many ways to earn money but it does not make sense if you haven't learned any idea of money management and grow your wealth.

Over time, we find changes in technology, health care, or practically anything you can think of. However, the education system in most parts of the world hasn't changed much. We are still learning the way our parents did when they were of our age.

In the traditional curriculum, there was no subject of money.

Forget about other courses, even the business courses don't consist of this topic.

What would you think if you saw a 6-year-old with a $100 bill? Wouldn't you freak out most probably? You would think who's stupid enough to give a child such a big sum of cash, wouldn't you?

Sadly, it has meant that no children should learn about money from a young age itself. We miss out on the opportunity to learn about one of the most essential tools mankind has ever created.

Ask your teachers whether they learned about money when they were small?

I'm sure the answer would be no for many of them.

Why would you want to educate a concept to others which you yourself had not learned earlier?

Instead of teaching us about Money, Schools instruct us to become a good employee. They don't educate us on how to make money work for us, instead they teach us how to work for it through hard labor.

Landing yourself in your dream job is harder than ever. There are a lot of candidates fighting the same.

Also, many companies aren't as loyal to their employees as they used to be. An employee can get fired anytime, without knowing what their fault was.

Unfortunately, a lot of schools still believe that landing & holding a job isn't a problem, so teach accordingly.

You're Not Late to Learn About Money

You might be wondering if it is too late for you to learn about money. But let me tell you, it's never too late.

Yes, that's right!

Irrespective of whether you are in a school or at a job, its concept is still worthy.

Even if you think you are too old for this, you could always teach this to your loved ones. Perhaps they will find it valuable.

CHAPTER 6

MAKING MONEY WORK FOR YOU

Making Money work for you is not a easy task to learn, experiencing losses, bullied, and other major factors that makes you lose focus is a very big deal when it comes to making the money work for you, especially when you don't have a lot of money.

After a Year of working with my father, my brothers and I had some money served for business. We saved the money so we can start doing our own thing.

One day a lady came with a proposal of farming, she had a friend who had a very big farm.

"Am looking for people who I can work with in farming for I and my friend have a farm we need to cultivate." She said.

"This is brilliant, we will think about it. We will give you an answer tomorrow." My brother said.

The all night we were thinking, talking and making plans of how it should be done. The oldest brother of mine had some experience in farming and gardening so we had no issues when it came to that.

The next morning, we went to her house. "We thought about it and realized we're ready to work with you." We said.

"We have everything prepared for you, you don't have to worry, pack your clothes and I'll take you to the farm tomorrow." She said.

We went to the farm and as we reached, we found out it wasn't even far from where we lived, it was a very big plot and there was a school at the same plot.

We were given one of the school offices where to sleep and live. We were not very surprised, but we were a bit heartbroken when it came to the sleeping arrangements, we were told everything is there, but the four (4) of us were given a single mattress, not double, but single. So, some of us slept on the floor until two weeks when they brought another single mattress for us.

"We have all the money prepared, we will buy everything needed, the only thing you have to do, is work very hard to never disappoint us for we will provide you with all that is needed." The own of the farm said.

We began to prepare the land for cultivating, it wasn't easy and after three days, we finished one part of the land and planted the seeds they bought.

Two weeks later

Vegetables grew, and we needed some fertilizers and chemicals needed to grow them in a healthy way.

"We don't have the money for all that as at now. Use what you have and it'll be paid to you after the sales of what you've cultivated." He said.

We began to use the served money and the same situation continued for about a month. The money we had finished as we bought what we needed for the treatment of the garden, and when they had they could also buy but not enough as they promised.

Things changed and we were not allowed to use electricity, playing music, watching TV, using the computer and so on.

After selling the stuffs for the first time, we went so we can discuss the deductions of the money we spent. He disagreed and said we will share the money equally.

"This is my land, and I am a poster, I know God and I know that he loves being equal, I've given you the land so that you can do whatever you want with it and make any profits you want. Keep working and we will share. The Land is yours." He said.

We we're shocked, but not too much for we knew we will get everything done and have much profits.

The man who called himself a Man of God, began to change and acting differently.

"I don't trust you, You're stealing the money whenever you sell, you're not trustworthy. Am changing the one who should be keeping the money. I'll be keeping it. We're opening a new account" He said.

"No, we agreed and you said this farm has been given to us, why are you taking it back now, before the finish of everything?" we asked.

"As I said, all of you aren't trustworthy, I can't give my land to people I don't trust." He said.

I felt puzzled, I didn't understand what was happening. My brothers were shocked and upset, so we agreed on just selling what remained and go.

The next morning he came with the lady who brought us to his farm. "Guys, I humbly apologize for what happened yesterday, I never thought of it my humble request of forgiveness to you. Let us continue and make something out of this." He said.

We continued working and selling. But things were not going well still, we had many differences and One day:

"I don't want you here, am cutting everything you've cultivated and give it to animals, pack your bags and leave tomorrow morning." He said.

We packed just as he said, in the morning my brother went to look for a car and we remained selling stuffs for the last time.

We never made the money we wanted to make, and that's how we lost our Money, the money we served for business.

We shared what we made out of gardening with him, and the money we got out of it, can't even buy a trouser. Why have I share this story with you? Why is it so vital for you to know this?

Note: When you have some money served, or you're serving the money. It's always important to know who you should work with, Know where to invest it and where you can make profit, instead of losing both your reputation, power, Energy and Money.

There are many ways you can make the Money work for you if you invest it correctly. I never thought about all these things as I was making my first investment, I never had time to learn or anyone to teach me what you're going to learn today in this chapter.

Money is a tool that can help you to achieve your goals. It can provide comfort and stability for your family, make it easier to plan for the future, and allow you to save towards important milestones. But to achieve these things, you need to know how to make your money work for you.

What Does It Mean To Make Your Money Work For You?

Making your money work for you means taking control of your finances, then using that control to continuously improve your financial stability and security.

You may eventually be able to gain financial independence or build wealth through investing. But neither of those things can happen without first understanding where your money is going and learning better ways to use it.

- ### Invest in your financial education

You have probably heard the popular saying that "knowledge is power."

While knowledge in itself (without action) is ineffectual, success begins with knowledge.

Investing in education gives you an unfair advantage over others.

Therefore, to achieve your clearly defined wealth-building goals, you need to invest in your financial education.

"Money is one form of power. But what is more powerful is financial education. Money comes and goes, but if you have the education about how money works, you gain power over it and can begin building wealth. The reason positive thinking alone does not work is because most people went to school and never learned how money works, so they spend their lives working for money."

"If you understand how money can work for and against you, you can make better decisions." "Financial literacy is not about wealth but about understanding money regardless of the amount. It's about how you treat it and how you maximise opportunities."

To let your money work for you, you must build the habit of consistently learning how money works.

- **Create a Budget**

As dull as it may sound, creating and sticking to a monthly expense plan is key to making your money grow. It not only helps to determine where you are spending your income but also helps you to change the way you manage your money. The ultimate goal is to spend less than you earn and keep track of where unnecessary expenditure is being made.

Budgeting isn't a one-time action; it is a continuous process of engaging with your expenditure habits every day. It involves:

Cutting out bad financial habits

Keeping a track of miscellaneous expenses

Drawing up monthly limits for different categories of spending

The idea is to keep a track of where your money goes in order to control it sensibly. If done right, budgeting is the real first step towards financial stability.

- ## Getting Out of Debt

More than anything, getting out of debt means finding ways to make your money work for you. Whether it's more robust savings tactics or new repayments strategies, there are options. So if you want to take the burden of debt off of your shoulders, here are some methods to try out.

It's easy to say you need to pay off a debt. But it's another thing actually to have the money for it. So before you cut down your expenses, you may need to save up first. A high-yield savings account is an available option that can help you build wealth to meet your financial goals.

Selecting a Debt Repayment Strategy

What do you think of when you hear the words "snowflake," "snowball," and "avalanche"? Perhaps you picture snow-capped mountains or blustery winter sports. But they're the names for some of the most popular debt repayment strategies. While these strategies encourage individuals to make additional payments on some of their debts, making the minimum payments on all debt is important.

The snowflake method encourages individuals to put any extra cash earned toward debt repayment. Any time there's excess to play with, you put it towards your debt. Since that helps you pay over your monthly minimum, you'll eventually finish off the debt. You can earn additional money in any way that works for you. For example, some people get side hustles on the weekend, or you can try selling items you don't want anymore.

What to Do With Extra Money

With the snowball strategy, you pay off your debts from smallest to largest, when evaluating the total amount owed. During this, you still make minimum payments on all your other debts. While it's motivating to see some of your financial troubles disappear, this may not work for you. The snowball method ignores interest rates, which gives a chance for other debts to grow.

On the other hand, the avalanche method works on the debts with the highest interest rates first. Unsecured debts, like credit card balances and personal loans, often come with unfavorable interest terms. Leaving them alone allows your debt to grow exponentially when you're not looking. Focusing on debts with the highest interest rate first could help you escape debt quickly and potentially spend less in interest overall.

- **Set up an emergency fund**

One way to avoid new debts is to have an emergency fund where you can take money to meet unexpected expenses.

An emergency fund is a stash of money put aside to cater to unplanned expenses (a car repair, for example) and unexpected circumstances (job loss, uninsured medical situations).

Most of the debts people incur are the result of some unplanned expenses or circumstances. However, instead of borrowing (at a usually high interest rate) to meet those emergencies, an emergency fund allows you to overcome them with the cash you have saved up — with no interest payments to a lender.

Before you let your money work for you through investing, set up an emergency fund equal to six months of your living expenses (your basic needs or your basic needs plus wants, as per the 50:30:20 budgeting approach). If your monthly living expenses amount to $7,000, for example, you'll need $42,000 in your emergency fund.

Why should this take priority over investing?

If an emergency arises, and you don't have an emergency fund, you may have to sell your investments when the market is on an uptrend (and miss all those gains) or on a downtrend (and take a loss on your investment).

Which should come first, paying off your debt or setting up an emergency fund?

It's best to set up your emergency fund in part (maybe three months of your living expenses) before cutting down your debts (you will still have to make minimum required payments on all debts). This is because if you focus solely on paying off debt and an emergency arises, you will still have to take on more debt.

Once you have some money in your emergency fund, focus on paying off your debt (with the debt snowballing approach) and come back to complete your emergency fund.

- Invest in the Stock Market

Your best choice is to invest in the stock market by buying individual ETFs (exchange-traded funds) and mutual funds in a "model portfolio" if you want to grow your money genuinely.

The fundamental idea is straightforward: Set aside at least 10% of your gross income. Put your money in long-term investments and let compound interest take care of the rest.

For instance, if you have $10,000 to start with, save $1,000 every month and put that money into a portfolio that would generate 10%. You would have $2.3 million after 30 years.

Your starting point as a beginner to forex trading

The foreign exchange market, also known as the forex market, is the world's most traded financial market. We're committed to ensuring our clients have the best education, tools, platforms, and accounts to navigate this market where to start when it comes to forex, you're in the right place. You'll find everything you need to know about forex trading, what it is, how it works and how to start trading.

What is forex?

Forex is short for foreign exchange – the transaction of changing one currency into another currency. This process can be performed for a variety of reasons including commercial, tourism and to enable international trade.

Forex is traded on the forex market, which is open to buy and sell currencies 24 hours a day, five days a week and is used by banks, businesses, investment firms, hedge funds and retail traders.

What is the forex market?

The forex market is by far the largest and most liquid financial market in the world, with an estimated average global daily turnover of more than US$6.5 trillion — which has risen from $5 trillion just a few years ago.

One critical feature of the forex market is that there is no central marketplace or exchange in a central location, as all trading is done electronically via computer networks. This is known as an over the counter (OTC) market.

Learn how to become a forex trader with our comprehensive guide. Become Financially stable with Forex. Get started here, www.winwithleon.com

Forex offers many benefits to retail traders.

You can trade around the clock in different sessions across the globe, as the forex market is not traded through a central exchange like a stock market. This means you can jump on volatility, wherever it happens. High liquidity also enables you to execute your orders quickly and effortlessly.

Trading forex using leverage allows you to open a position by putting up only a portion of the full trade value. You can also go long (buy) or short (sell) depending on whether you think a forex pair's value will rise or fall.

Forex trading offers constant opportunities across a wide range of FX pairs. FXTM's comprehensive range of educational resources are a perfect way to get started and improve your trading knowledge.

Understanding Currency Pairs

All transactions made on the forex market involve the simultaneous buying and selling of two currencies.

This 'currency pair' is made up of a base currency and a quote currency, whereby you sell one to purchase another. The price for a pair is how much of the quote currency it costs to buy one unit of the base currency. You can make a profit by correctly forecasting the price move of a currency pair.

FXTM offers hundreds of combinations of currency pairs to trade including the majors which are the most popular traded pairs in the forex market. These include the Euro against the US Dollar, the US Dollar against the Japanese Yen and the British Pound against the US Dollar.

For most currency pairs, a pip is the fourth decimal place, the main exception being the Japanese Yen where a pip is the second decimal place.

On the forex market, trades in currencies are often worth millions, so small bid-ask price differences (i.e. several pips) can soon add up to a significant profit. Of course, such large trading volumes mean a small spread can also equate to significant losses.

Trading forex is risky, so always trade carefully and implement risk management tools and techniques. Get started with Forex at www.winwithleon.com

CHAPTER 7

A JOB CAN'T GIVE FINANCIAL FFREEDOM

After coming back home from the farm without money, I began searching for a Job again. It took me 3 months to find it. In the morning, I received a call from my brother in-law. He told me they needed an assistant in the construction company he was working with.

The same day I went for interviews, and they accepted me with a condition of staying at the company house which was being constructed and safeguard storage of materials that were brought for the construction of the building.

I agreed and started working. I was staying with a friend, there was no electricity in the house and the building was unfinished.

I used to work too hard and my boss never respected me at all. He never respected his workers and insulted everyone, there was no time to rest. I used to work even on weekends. Working extra time and not getting paid for it.

I wasted too much of my time working so hard and getting paid less. I started comparing people who work for money, (which meant myself at that time) with people who make their money work for them and found a very huge difference.

I didn't get enough that I worked for, and one day my Job Ended. I remained unemployed without making even half of what can make a person Rich.

I realized working for money won't make you Rich.

Why A Job can't make you successful

Getting a job and trading your time for money may seem like a good idea. There's only one problem with it. It's one of the stupidest way you can possibly generate income! This is truly income for dummies.

Why is getting a job so dumb? Because you only get paid when you're working. Don't you see a problem with that, why should you only have money after working hard and tired? or have you been so thoroughly brainwashed into thinking it's reasonable and intelligent to only earn income when you're working?

Have you never considered that it might be better to be paid even when you're not working? Who taught you that you could only earn income while working? Some other brainwashed employee?

Don't you think your life would be much easier if you got paid while you were eating, sleeping, and playing with the kids too? Why not get paid 24/7? Get paid whether you work or not. Don't your plants grow even when you aren't tending to them? Why not your bank account?

Who cares how many hours you work? Only a handful of people on this entire planet care how much time you spend at the office. Most of us won't even notice whether you work 6 hours a week or 60.

But if you have something of value to provide that matters to us, most of us will be happy to pull out our wallets and pay you for it. We don't care about your time — we only care enough to pay for the value we receive. Do you really care how long it took me to write this? Would you pay me twice as much if it took me 8 hours?

Non-dummies often start out on the traditional income for dummies path. So don't feel bad if you're just now realizing you've been suckered. Non-dummies eventually realize that trading time for money is indeed extremely dumb and that there must be a better way. And of course there is a better way. The key is to de-couple your value from your time.

Smart people build systems that generate income 24/7, especially passive income. This can include starting a business, building a web site, becoming an investor, or generating royalty income from creative work.

The system delivers the ongoing value to people and generates income from it, and once it's in motion, it runs continuously whether you tend to it or not. From that moment on, the bulk of your time can be invested in increasing your income (by refining your system or spawning new ones) instead of merely maintaining your income. Build a website at www.winwithleon.com and Make passive income.

This web site is an example of such a system. You can sell stuff for big companies and make money, or write blogs. The web server delivers the value, and other systems (most of which I didn't even build and don't even understand) collect income and deposit it automatically into my bank account. But of course it cost me a lot of money to launch this business, right? Um, yeah, $9 is an awful lot these days (to register the domain name). Everything after that was profit.

Sure it takes some upfront time and effort to design and implement your own income-generating systems. But you don't have to reinvent the wheel — feel free to use existing systems like ad networks and affiliate programs. Once you get going, you won't have to work so many hours to support yourself.

Wouldn't it be nice to be out having dinner with your spouse, knowing that while you're eating, you're earning money? If you want to keep working long hours because you enjoy it, go right ahead. If you want to sit around doing nothing, feel free. As long as your system continues delivering value to others, you'll keep getting paid whether you're working or not.

Your local bookstore is filled with books containing workable systems others have already designed, tested, and debugged. Nobody is born knowing how to start a business or generate investment income, but you can easily learn it, the more you learn the more you'll Earn.

How long it takes you to figure it out is irrelevant because the time is going to pass anyway. You might as well emerge at some future point as the owner of income-generating systems as opposed to a lifelong wage slave. This isn't all or nothing. If your system only generates a few hundred dollars a month, that's a significant step in the right direction.

Limited experience

You might think it's important to get a job to gain experience. But that's like saying you should play tennis to get experience playing tennis. You gain experience from living, regardless of whether you have a job or not.

A job only gives you experience at that job, but you gain "experience" doing just about anything, so that's no real benefit at all. Sit around doing nothing for a couple years, and you can call yourself an experienced meditator, philosopher, or politician.

The problem with getting experience from a job is that you usually just repeat the same limited experience over and over. You learn a lot in the beginning and then stagnate. This forces you to miss other experiences that would be much more valuable.

And if your limited skill set ever becomes obsolete, then your experience won't be worth squat. In fact, ask yourself what the experience you're gaining right now will be worth in 20-30 years. Will your job even exist then?

Consider this. Which experience would you rather gain? The knowledge of how to do a specific job really well — one that you can only monetize by trading your time for money — or the knowledge of how to enjoy financial abundance for the rest of your life without ever needing a job again? Now I don't know about you, but I'd rather have the latter experience. That seems a lot more useful in the real world, wouldn't you say?

Lifelong domestication

Getting a job is like enrolling in a human domestication program. You learn how to be a good pet.

Look around you. Really look. What do you see? Are these the surroundings of a free human being? Or are you living in a cage for unconscious animals? Have you fallen in love with the color beige?

How's your obedience training coming along? Does your master reward your good behavior? Do you get disciplined if you fail to obey your master's commands?

Is there any spark of free will left inside you? Or has your conditioning made you a pet for life?

Humans are not meant to be raised in cages. Don't allow your job to make you lose Freedom. You poor thing...

Begging for money

When you want to increase your income, do you have to sit up and beg your master for more money? Does it feel good to be thrown some extra Scooby Snacks now and then?

Or are you free to decide how much you get paid without needing anyone's permission but your own?

If you have a business and one customer says "no" to you, you simply say "next."

Loss of freedom

It takes a lot of effort to tame a human being into an employee. The first thing you have to do is break the human's independent will. A good way to do this is to give them a weighty policy manual filled with nonsensical rules and regulations.

This leads the new employee to become more obedient, fearing that he/she could be disciplined at any minute for something incomprehensible. Thus, the employee will likely conclude it's safest to simply obey the master's commands without question. Stir in some office politics for good measure, and we've got a freshly minted mind slave.

As part of their obedience training, employees must be taught how to dress, talk, move, and so on. We can't very well have employees thinking for themselves, now can we? That would ruin everything.

God forbid you should put a plant on your desk when it's against the company policy. Oh no, it's the end of the world! Leon has a plant on his desk! Jonathan the enforcers! Send Leon back for another round of sterility training!

Free human beings think such rules and regulations are silly of course. The only policy they need is: "Be smart. Be nice. Do what you love. Have fun."

Becoming a coward

Have you noticed that employed people have an almost endless capacity to whine about problems at their companies? But they don't really want solutions — they just want to vent and make excuses why it's all someone else's fault.

It's as if getting a job somehow drains all the free will out of people and turns them into spineless cowards. If you can't call your boss a jerk now and then without fear of getting fired, you're no longer free. You've become your master's property.

When you work around cowards all day long, don't you think it's going to rub off on you? Of course it will. It's only a matter of time before you sacrifice the noblest parts of your humanity on the altar of fear: first courage… then honesty… then honor and integrity… and finally your independent will.

You sold your humanity for nothing but an Illusion. And now your greatest fear is discovering the truth of what you've become.

I don't care how badly you've been beaten down. It is never too late to regain your courage. Never!

Happily jobless

What's the alternative to getting a job? The alternative is to remain happily jobless for life and to generate income through other means. Realize that you earn income by providing value — not time — so find a way to provide your best value to others, and charge a fair price for it.

One of the simplest and most accessible ways is to start your own business. Whatever work you'd otherwise do via employment, find a way to provide that same value directly to those who will benefit most from it. It takes a bit more time to get going, but your freedom is easily worth the initial investment of time and energy. Then you can buy your own Scooby Snacks for a change.

And of course everything you learn along the way, you can share with others to generate even more value. So even your mistakes can be monetized.

One of the greatest fears you'll confront is that you may not have any real value to offer others. Maybe being an employee and getting paid by the hour is the best you can do. Maybe you just aren't worth that much.

That line of thinking is all just part of your conditioning. It's absolute nonsense. As you begin to dump such brainwashing, you'll soon recognize that you have the ability to provide enormous value to others and that people will gladly pay you for it. There's only one thing that prevents you from seeing this truth — fear.

All you really need is the courage to be yourself. Your real value is rooted in who you are, not what you do. The only thing you need actually do is express your real self to the world. You've been told all sort of lies as to why you can't do that. But you'll never know true happiness and fulfillment until you summon the courage to do it anyway.

The next time someone says to you, "Get a job," I suggest you reply as I did: "No, please... not that! Anything but that!" Then poke them right in the eyes, lol just Kidding on that.

You already know deep down that getting a job isn't what you want. So don't let anyone try to tell you otherwise. Learn to trust your inner wisdom, even if the whole world says you're wrong and foolish for doing so. Years from now you'll look back and realize it was one of the best decisions you ever made.

I only came to this realization after countless nights of study in a place where you lose yourself in a pulse of books.

When I started my career, I believed that the way to get rich was to study hard, get a good job, and work my way up the corporate ladder. I thought that if I put in enough hours, I could get promoted to a great position that paid six figures and have the life of my dreams.

Work to Learn, Not to Earn

When Warren Buffett graduated from Columbia University, he offered to go work for free at the investment firm of his teacher and mentor, Benjamin Graham.

Why would someone who loves money so much offer to work for free? Why wouldn't he be trying to get the job with the highest salary like most of us do when we graduate?

Because Buffett knew that working there would make him far richer than any regular job could do. Not because of a salary, but because of the knowledge he would gain about how to make money in the stock market.

Buffett realized that a salary was a drop in the bucket next to what could be made by putting Grahams' value investing techniques to use.

He knew he couldn't get rich on a salary alone, so he looked for ways to increase his knowledge and skill to focus on his long-term goal of building wealth.

Although many of us are not in a position to work for free, we can still keep this story in mind when making decisions in our lives. It may be better long term to work somewhere like a startup, even with a lower salary, but that offers you the chance to increase your knowledge so that you can start your own company in the future. Or you may find a way to work for free in your spare time to learn something valuable, either for someone else or for yourself.

Despite all the pressure to move up the corporate ladder, at some point, you need to realize that it isn't the job of your boss or your company to make you rich. Their job is to pay you fairly for the work you do, nothing more. If you want to make more money, you will likely have to sacrifice more for the company by taking on more responsibility that will start to take away more of your free time.

It is also very easy as you move up the corporate ladder to keep increasing your living standard. Raises and promotions encourage us to buy bigger houses, nicer cars, expensive watches, even a boat or jetski, for heaven's sake! Buying all these flashy things makes us look rich, but it prevents us from building wealth.

If you want to get rich, you have to do it on your terms. You have to learn about investing or starting a business and then take the money you earn from your day job to build something worthwhile in your spare time. This could be a side business, a stock portfolio, or a collection of real estate.

Over time and with diligence, your investment portfolio or side business will become more valuable than your job, and you will find yourself achieving financial security or even independence.

I've spent most of my free time over the past several years learning about School, Education system, Jobs and Life. So, I've Built a University, THE WALK TO FINANCIAL FREEDOM which has allowed me to teach what I learned and educate other people about the type and kind of education system they should invest in. This University grew my equity at high rates of return and provide a nice monthly cash flow to supplement my salary.

I could not have accomplished this if I had spent all my extra time focused on my day job trying to get a higher salary from a Boss that never respected me and my time.

Enroll in THE WALK TO FINANCIAL FREEDOM University at www.winwithleon.com

CHAPTER 8

BUILDING A BUSINESS

Starting a business requires a lot of work. The amount of documentation, legal requirements, and strategic development can simply be overwhelming. But without putting in the effort, you'll struggle to turn your idea into a successful business.

Now, I'm not looking to scare you away from entrepreneurship. I just want to keep things realistic, while telling you that it is 100% possible to start your own business. It's going to take time, effort, and potentially a few setbacks, but you can do it.

At this point, you may be wondering where to start. Should you work on your business name and logo or tackle your business structure? Does it make sense to already start applying for loans or focus on product development?

It can be difficult to know the right steps to take. But that's ok. Starting your own venture is all about trial and error. Working through the process to find what works for you and what resonates with potential customers.

But rather than being overwhelmed by all the decisions and tasks you have at hand, there are steps you can take to kickstart the development of your business. Let's get started.

Know yourself as an entrepreneur before you start

Starting a business is a process that requires an enormous amount of thought and careful examination. First, you need to take a good look at your strengths, weaknesses and skills. This will allow you to start thinking about what you can do and what you cannot do.

It is important to start here even if you already have world's best business idea, because you might not have the skills or personality traits to enable you to make it into a successful business. You want to come up with business ideas where you are naturally best suited to be successful, for example:

A person with a decent level of programming skill is well adapted to starting a web development agency.

A person that has a short attention span might not want to consider accountancy related businesses.

An person that doesn't enjoy speaking to new people wouldn't consider a heavily client facing business.

These are just three general examples, but it gives you an idea of the thought process. The crucial point is to understand yourself and your team, and if you are well suited to any business ideas, areas of business or specific types of business. It allows you to start coming up with ideas and narrowing down what businesses you could start.

Before you start a business, you should be absolutely clear about why you are doing it. That may sound obvious, but there are actually many reasons why someone should choose to turn their back on the security of a job and career for the uncertainty of starting a business. So the clearer you are about what exactly you are trying to achieve, the better chance you have of achieving it.

Wealth, power, fame, saving the world? Most entrepreneurs are motivated by a mix of the above although most wouldn't like to admit it. Understanding what is driving you to start a business is a major factor in determining what type of business you should start. Why? Because when a business you start isn't aligned with personal ambition, it is much more likely you will fail.

You should make sure from the beginning that your personal goals and drive are compatible with your business, for example:

Someone who seeks wealth might want to look at companies in the financial services industry, where Fintech valuations and revenues are typically much higher than other start-up businesses.

Someone who seeks power and influence could achieve this through any form of media business.

Someone who seeks out fame might be best suited to an entertainment related business.

Someone who wants to save the world might start a business tackling climate change through renewable energy.

It is important to understand why you are starting a business so you can focus on business ideas that will help you get to where you want to go.

While it is possible to create a successful business solely to make a lot of money, in reality, it will be hard work if there isn't at least one other factor acting as a motivator. This is because it can take many years between starting a business and receiving any money from it – if ever – and along the way the hard work required is immense, and the possibility of failure is very real.

Simply pinning your hopes on a future possible pot of gold is unlikely to be enough to sustain you through the difficult times. So make sure you have a good reason, work hard and enjoy the ride!

Step Guide to Establishing a profitable business

1. Be inspired. Your first step is to get inspired to be an entrepreneur. If you're reading this article, you're probably already there.

2. Have a passion. Few business owners are successful without a sufficient passion driving their efforts. Find something you're passionate about.

3. Educate yourself. You don't need a college degree, but you do need to be aware of the risks and realities of business ownership.

4. Generate an idea. This is the hard part: coming up with an idea that has the potential to launch a full-fledged business.

5. Preliminarily research the idea. Poke around the web and see what you can find. Are there other businesses like this?

6. Talk to others. See what your friends and family think about your idea, and be open to criticism.

7. Develop the idea. Brainstorm to work out the potential flaws and key advantages.

8. Research and start a business plan. Now's your chance to get more involved. Find out what competitors there are and dig deep to create a full-fledged business plan (use the next steps to help you).

9. Determine your target market. Not everyone will be your target customer. Find a niche.

10. Come up with a financial model. How much are you going to charge? How much will it cost to run the business? How profitable can you be?

11. Come up with an operations model. Who and what do you need to maintain production?

12. Come up with a staffing plan. Determine the people you need to hire to get things started.

13. Come up with a sales and marketing plan. This isn't superfluous. Sales and marketing are what will drive your business to grow.

14. Come up with a growth plan. How do you expect to scale in the first year? What about years two and three?

15. Decide on a legal structure for your business. Every legal construct has advantages and disadvantages. Think carefully about what will work best.

16. Determine what you need to start. Think about the people, resources and capital you need, and have both an "ideal" and "minimum" range.

17. Objectively analyze the risk. Determine how much you stand to lose if the company goes under.

18. If you're ready, quit your current job. If everything looks good, pull the trigger and invest yourself full-time in your enterprise.

19. Secure capital. Withdraw savings, borrow from friends, seek funding or set up a line of credit with a bank – or some combination of these.

20. Seek resources and aid. Join a small-business development center and find local resources to help you succeed.

21. Scout for potential clients. Keep your eyes peeled for individuals and businesses that might buy from you, and the earlier the better. Try to get at least one client before investing a dime.

22. Register your business name. It's a simple step, but a necessary one.

23. Get a tax ID. Don't forget about your tax responsibilities.

24. File for state and local taxes. Don't neglect this financial step.

25. Obtain any necessary permits or licenses. Your business may require additional legal registrations.

26. Recruit one or more mentors. Find experienced entrepreneurs who can help you with the remaining steps, offering insight and guidance.

27. Find your key locations. Your office location, operations HQ and related issues are important decisions to make.

28. Establish a unique brand. Find out what makes your business unique, and develop a brand around it.

29. Start building a personal brand. While you're at it, build a personal brand for yourself.

30. Create a test product or service. Call it a prototype if you want. Create a sample if you haven't already.

31. Establish key vendors and partners. Find contractors, vendors and suppliers to help your business succeed.

32. Learn and apply your employer responsibilities. You'll have to offer certain benefits, conditions and withholdings.

33. Hire your first employees. Hire the bare minimum you need to get started.

34. Create a human resource plan and company culture. Create some guidelines, and hire people who will adhere to them.

35. Start selling. Go out and sell the heck out of your products.

36. Launch a website. As soon as you can, establish an online presence.

37. Outline and begin a digital marketing campaign. Digital marketing is cheap, easy, and effective. SEO, content marketing, and social media are good places to start.

38. Network everywhere you go. Make it a point to meet people. You never know who could be a new client or employee.

39. Find at least one dependable, long-term client. Prioritize getting at least one surefire long-term client.

40. Use promotions and discounts to attract new customers. Profitability is not as important as recognition in your early stages.

41. Learn from customer feedback and launch a second iteration of your products or services. Make tweaks to your offerings.

42. Hire more employees if necessary. When you're ready, expand the team.

43. Tweak your operations to become more efficient. No operation plan is perfect. Find ways to improve yours.

44. Ensure your cash flow remains positive, with proper safety measures. Cash can kill an otherwise profitable business. Don't neglect it.

45. Scale your sales strategy. Do more.

46. Scale your marketing strategy. Reach further.

47. Invest in infrastructural improvements. Improve whatever you can afford to improve to make your customers happier.

48. Learn more about your industry. Reach out to competitors, and attend industry conferences.

49. Become a thought leader. Establish yourself as an authority by speaking, writing and hosting webinars.

50. Evaluate your progress thus far, and adjust your business plan. Determine where you are in contrast to where you thought you'd be, and think about what expectations you had that were wrong. Revisit your business plan and adjust it to reflect your current situation and understandings.

Every business is unique, so yours may not perfectly adhere to the formula. Use these steps as a loose guideline for the course of your business' development, and thrust yourself into the process as much as you can.

CHAPTER 9

IMPORTANCE OF ENTREPRENEURSHIP

Entrepreneurship Accelerates Economic Growth

By creating new products and services, they stimulate new employment, which ultimately results in the acceleration of economic development. So public policy that encourages and supports entrepreneurship should be considered important for economic growth.

Entrepreneurship can be considered a national asset, and entrepreneurs are the drivers of that asset for any country. It is a dynamic process that not only increases wealth and but can also create value that results in improved well-being.

Entrepreneurship plays an important role in changing society, so it makes sense to cultivate, motivate, and remunerate this greatest asset to the greatest extent possible.

In entrepreneurship, unutilized resources, labor, and capital are utilized most efficiently. Entrepreneurs take on risks in the hopes of making profit, or in the case of social entrepreneurship, of solving a problem facing communities. So the significance of entrepreneurs and the role of entrepreneurship go beyond the business world. The importance of entrepreneurship is so broad that it's quite tough to explain all the aspects of it in a short blog post. However, I would like to shed some light on the importance and role of entrepreneurship in economic development and society.

By creating new products and services, they stimulate new employment, which ultimately results in the acceleration of economic development. So public policy that encourages and supports entrepreneurship should be considered important for economic growth.

A large number of new jobs and opportunities are created by entrepreneurship. Entrepreneurship creates a huge amount of entry-level jobs that are very much important to turn unskilled jobholders into skilled ones. It also prepares and provides experienced workers to large industries. The increase in the total employment of a country largely depends on the rise of entrepreneurship. So the role of entrepreneurship in creating new job opportunities is huge.

By bringing innovation to every aspect of businesses, entrepreneurial ventures enhance production utilizing the existing resources in the most effective ways. Entrepreneurs develop new markets by introducing new and improved products, services, and technology. Thus, they help generate new wealth and add more to the national income. So the government can offer the citizens more national benefits.

Entrepreneurship is a blanket term related to starting a business. Entrepreneurship is the "pursuit of opportunity beyond resources controlled," considering it as a kind of managerial approach rather than a specific time, like a business's creation, or a specific person within a business, such as its founder.

While there are some complicating factors to the relationship between entrepreneurship, economic growth, development, and welfare, discussed below, the increase in economic growth from entrepreneurship is considerable.

It is not, however, a magic bullet, and as discussed below broader economic conditions outside of entrepreneurship are important in determining whether economic growth occurs.

Why you should become an Entrepreneur

Deciding to start your own business is a leap of faith. It requires pushing out of your comfort zone and trying something new. If that idea excites you, why wait around? You're ready to take the leap and be the CEO of your OWN COMPANY. It's a lot of work and there are some risks, but the potential for rewards is huge. If you're not convinced yet, here are some of the best reasons for starting your own business.

- Each day at the office will be motivating.

When you're working for someone else, it can be tough to find the motivation to do the best possible work. No matter how much work you put in, the owners of the company will get the ultimate rewards.

When you're your own boss, you'll find motivation at work every day. Following your dreams is exciting, and you're in control of your own success. The day-to-day vitality of your business depends on you, so you'll be driven to make each day as productive as you can. You'll know that your own hard work and drive will help you reap the rewards, and that'll keep the fire burning in your belly to make each day count.

You'll be following your passions.

Many entrepreneurs start their own business to follow their dreams and fulfill their passion. Following your dreams will fulfill you in a way that working for someone else may not do. You are in charge of creating your business from the ground up, so you can shape your company to be something you're proud of and that you may even be able to pass on to your children as your legacy.

- You can pursue social justice or support non-profits.

One of the most fulfilling parts of becoming an entrepreneur is setting up your company for social gain. You can opt to support non-profits, charities, or community efforts with your profits. Or you can set up your business to solve a problem in your community or in the world at large – whatever your passion may be.

For example, consider Snowday, a company started by teach-turned-entrepreneur Jordyn Lexton. It's a food truck, but it's doing more than just filling the hungry bellies of passersby. Snowday employs young people that have been incarcerated (which makes it harder for them to find work) and helps them gain valuable skills and experience on the job. Starting your own business gives you a unique opportunity to make the world a better place.

- You can achieve financial independence

Many people commit to starting a business with the dream of financial comfort. While it's true that getting your company off the ground can take grit and result in some lean times while you're getting started, the ultimate goal of being your own boss is cultivating financial independence.

With determination and hard work, there's no cap on how lucrative your own business can be. If you aspire to build wealth, there's no reason why you can't achieve that goal.

Starting your own business has several financial benefits over working for a wage or salary. First, you're building an enterprise that has the potential for growth – and your wallet grows as your company does. Second, your business itself is a valuable asset. As your business grows, it's worth more and more. You may decide to sell it or you may hold on to it and pass it down to your heirs. Either way, it's valuable.

- You can control your lifestyle and your schedule.

Perhaps you've spent years in the corporate world and you feel ready to turn over a new leaf after years of reporting to a superior. Starting your own business can give you a more flexible lifestyle and schedule so you don't feel like you're running in circles on that corporate hamster wheel.

You can opt to schedule meetings around your family schedule or you can opt to work from home – the sky's the limit when you're the boss. You still have to get the work done, but nobody's looking over your shoulder making sure you do it their way on their time.

Starting a business is hard work, and that flexible schedule may not happen right away. Even if you're working long hours, however, you know that you're doing it for yourself and your family and not for a distant boss or shareholder.

- You can start from scratch.

This is your business! You make the rules. You're not restricted by the standards and procedures of your boss or corporate culture. You can offer a product or a service that fits your vision. You can also build your company according to your own ideas.

Maybe you've thought of a way to make processes more efficient. Maybe you want to make sure your employees get fair wages and family leave time. Whatever problems you've encountered in the working world, you have a chance to do something different with your own business.

Many entrepreneurs say that once they've sampled the freedom of being their own boss and calling the shots at running their own company, they'd never want to work for someone else again.

- You'll get tax benefits.

Starting your own business takes funding and it may take some time to turn a profit, but you can start taking advantage of some substantial tax breaks right off the bat.

Government programs support small business entrepreneurship and seek to reward these endeavors with impressive tax incentives. You'll want to work with a financial planner or an accountant to make sure you're setting up your business in a way that will allow you to get the benefit of these government programs.

Note that there are also a variety of programs aimed specifically at business started by women and minorities, so you may be able to get grant funding and other benefits to get your business off the ground.

- You'll have true job security.

The stress of climbing the corporate ladder is real. You never know whether you'll be promoted or whether you may be handed a pink slip – these life-altering decisions are in someone else's hands and beyond your control. When you start your own company, you know you're investing in your future and in your own job security.

Moreover, should you choose to start a family business, you could be providing jobs for other members of your family, as well. Your destiny is in your own hands – no more layoffs in your future.

- You'll become an expert at a broad range of skills.

Part of running your own business is learning to wear a lot of different hats, especially early on. You'll have to pick up a lot of new skills, from HR decisions to inventory management to customer service.

You'll soon become a pro in your own industry, as well as a pro at a variety of new skills you'll learn on the job. As your business develops, you'll continue to pick up new knowledge and abilities. You'll know how every tiny aspect of your operation works. You can't get that kind of experience anywhere else.

As your business grows, you may opt to continue manning the helm for those tasks you enjoy – whether that's graphic design or accounting – but you can outsource those tasks that you dread. You can also turn those skills to new tasks. Who knows? You may even want to start another business!

- You can be creative.

It's up to you to decide what your business will produce, sell, or which services it will offer – that's exciting! Rather than following the formula of those who came before you, you're looking at a chance to develop a concept or an idea that nobody else ever has.

Even if you stay mainstream with your product or service, each day as an entrepreneur allows you to find new, outside-the-book ways to problem solve. Innovation and creativity are necessary traits for a successful entrepreneur, and you'll hone those skills daily.

Knowing that each day brings new challenges, exciting opportunities, and a chance to engage your passion is reason enough to start your own business. Knowing that you've decided to take control of your own future is empowering. What are you waiting for? The time is now!

You can also become a successful online Entrepreneur, just like the way I started. I've built everything that can help you start from scratch until you build your own business online by building a successful website through the guide . It'll only take you a month to build a successful business online.

Transform Your Ideas into Profits.

Start a Business From 1+ Million Lucrative Niches.

We all have a hobby or something that gets us excited and motivated when we think about it. It only takes one idea to create a very successful business online. Don't have any ideas? No problem, We will help you choose a direction of your business from over 1,000,000 different niches.

Your Revenue Sources Are Unlimited.

598,500,000 Products YOU Can Instantly Sell.

Once you have traffic, you need to "make money" from this traffic. This is the fun part. Without spending a dime, you can promote all the top brands in the world through affiliate programs. As a member, you'll learn how you can choose from close to 600 MILLION products/services and easily promote them on your website. No inventory. No shipping. No support required.

Visit- www.winwithleon.com to get started today.

CHAPTER 10

STAYING RICH FOREVER

Once I realized the path to financial freedom, I found out the importance of Money management. Money management can make you Rich forever, because you'll never have to waste money on unnecessary things.

I realized the truth of life and began to love Entrepreneurship than a Job. This has made me find a way of continuing to live a successful life. Learning how to stay Rich forever is so important to you as an Entrepreneur.

If you want to stay wealthy for a lifetime and pass down wealth for future generations, you need a plan. Wealth managers have many approaches that they will customize for your specific situation and your wishes. But they almost all have similar themes that we can learn from.

"Making money is a hobby that will complement any other hobbies you have beautifully."

The terms "rich" and "wealthy" are often used interchangeably, but in fact they are two different concepts. Wealth relates to how much money you have in the bank, and the security of your assets.

To be rich, and stay rich, is more of an attitude, a state of mind that doesn't necessarily relate to your assets, but your quality of life.

However, if you're looking to turn a big paycheck or other assets (stocks, real estate, an inheritance, etc.) into lasting wealth, or "stay rich," you'll need to learn to manage your money, making careful choices to ensure your assets won't disappear when the going gets tough.

Of course, you can't take your money with you when you die, but you can follow certain steps to stay rich so that it lasts through your life.

- Diversify your finances in all areas of your life.

Diversification is not only the key to building wealth, it's also the key to sustaining the wealth that you have. Ensure that your money is well diversified across a broad spectrum of investment classes including stocks, bonds, mutual funds, real estate, and cash.

Different areas of the market will respond differently to the same event, so if you have invested in both stocks and bonds, for instance, your stocks may take a hit in a market swing, but you may compensate for the loss by a positive movement in the bond market.

Keep in mind that your risk objective may be different than when you were building wealth. You may now find capital preservation (keeping what you have) becoming more important than the risk that comes along with more aggressive (risky) investments.

- Understand the risk-return tradeoff.

This principle states that the higher the risk you take with an investment, the higher the potential return.

Determine your risk tolerance (how much you can safely afford to lose if the investment fails, how much time you have to recover from a potential loss) and talk to your financial adviser about how to balance your investments so that you get some return, but you don't risk financial ruin in the process.

- Keep liquidity in mind.

Liquidity refers to how quickly and easily an asset or security can be turned into another asset.

Cash is extremely liquid, while something like real estate is not. Although you can build a great deal of wealth "on paper" using real estate, you'll also find that it takes time to sell your real estate properties and convert them to cash.

If you think you'll ever need cash from your assets in a hurry, it's best not to park too much of that cash into real estate.

Learn more about diversification by reading How to Reduce Financial Risk.

- Invest in new opportunities.

You shouldn't stop trying to build wealth just because you're rich. Some of the richest people in the world are still making investments.

Now that you're rich, it's time to make money work for you instead of you working for money. Find business opportunities that you can invest in to build on the wealth that you have.

- Become an angel investor.

When you're an angel investor, you'll have the opportunity to invest in startups. You could become a part of the next Uber or Amazon.

This is also a way to "invest with your values" by investing in particular companies you believe in and supporting them in a more direct way.

- Make your money last.

Live on your income, not your liquidation of assets, or keep your spending within what is considered a safe zone. Many experts suggest keeping your spending under 5–6% of your liquid net worth each year.

Avoid liquidating your assets just to buy luxury items, otherwise you'll be a consumer who loses money and not an investor who earns money. Spending money on things that do not retain value or have no sentimental value is not a good way to make your money last.

- Develop a budget.

Yes, even if you're rich, you're going to need to live on a budget. This is for two reasons.

For starters, a budget is just as important for you if you're rich as it is for someone of lesser means, because it's easy to fall victim to the "bottomless pit" mindset. That's when you perceive that you have an infinite supply of money. As a result, you're more likely to burn through it and lose it. If you maintain a budget, you'll be in a better position to preserve your wealth.

A budget is a good idea for everybody. A budget forces you to itemize your spending and practice discipline with your hard-earned wealth.

- Avoid conspicuous consumption.

If you are showing off your wealth by purchasing a variety of luxury goods, it might be a good idea to think about whether you are doing this for genuine reasons or if you are doing so to prove something to others. You are more likely to preserve your wealth and feel fulfilled by not spending in this way.

- Set up a trust.

If you'd like to preserve your wealth for future generations, consider establishing a financial trust that will prevent spendthrift descendants from squandering away the money that you'd like to pass on to them.

"Trust places safeguards around how beneficiaries can access and spend the money that's been left to them."

You can also dictate how your money is spent in the future when you set up a trust. That's a great way to ensure that your wealth preservation strategies continue throughout future generations. You may set up a stipulation that the money in the trust can only be used for educational purposes, for instance, or that it will be dispensed in set a yearly or monthly sum.

"Be aware that once you place your assets in a trust, they are no longer considered to be your assets."

- Talk to a financial advisor.

Even though you're rich, you'll find that there are financial advisor who have a great deal of input about how you can manage your money in such a way that you'll preserve the wealth you worked hard to earn.

Financial advisers help you create a financial plan as well as manage your investments. They help you set goals and use your money in the ways that bring you satisfaction.

This person takes the holistic approach to help you wrap your arms around everything in your financial life. Your financial adviser can also help you find and be the "quarterback" for your other advisors (tax professional, estate attorney, etc.)

- Give back to society.

Now that you have money, do something good with some of it and you'll find that the laws of the universe work marvelously in your favor. One of the best ways to preserve your wealth is to be generous with the money that you have (and not just because of the tax break!).

There is a reason why rich families have their own foundations (for example, the Rockefeller Foundation). That's because they understand the importance of giving.

Words of appreciation

I therefore take this time to thank You, for the time, Energy, efforts and any investment you made to reading my book. It's not easy to become Financially free, But let me take this time to wish you the best of all as you go implement what you've learned, through out the courses of my story and advises from this Book.

As you begin to discover yourself and all that you're capable of, take time to reinforce your memory to everything you've Learned, you can be rest assured that you'll probably make it to the best extent you've always dreamed.

If you have no idea where to start from, I've outlined everything a d set up everything just for your. Build your business at www.winwithleon.com

With Love,

Leon

"The only locked doors are in your own Mind. Doors in reality, are open and all you have to do is walk through."